FASTING AND FEASTING

Text copyright © Gordon Giles 2008
The author asserts the moral right
to be identified as the author of this work

Published by
The Bible Reading Fellowship
15 The Chambers, Vineyard
Abingdon OX14 3FE
United Kingdom
Tel: +44 (0)1865 319700
Email: enquiries@brf.org.uk
Website: www.brf.org.uk

ISBN 978 1 84101 569 9
First published 2008
10 9 8 7 6 5 4 3 2 1 0

Acknowledgments
Unless otherwise stated, scripture quotations are taken from The New Revised
Standard Version of the Bible, Anglicized Edition, copyright © 1989, 1995 by the
Division of Christian Education of the National Council of the Churches of Christ
in the USA, and are used by permission. All rights reserved.

Extracts from The Book of Common Prayer of 1662, the rights of which are
vested in the Crown in perpetuity within the United Kingdom, are reproduced by
permission of Cambridge University Press, Her Majesty's Printers.

A catalogue record for this book is available from the British Library

Printed in Singapore by Craft Print International Ltd

Gordon Giles

Daily Bible readings from Ash Wednesday to Easter Day

FASTING AND FEASTING

Acknowledgments

It was my good fortune in the summer of 2007 to have a period of study leave, during which I was able to research and write this book. It is not easy to lay down the reins of parish life, and impossible without the cooperation and support of so many people. So I must record my thanks to Bishop Peter Wheatley and Father Richard Knowling, who made a sabbatical possible, and to The Reverends Jackie Fish, Barry Oakley and Reg Dunn, who held the fort while I was away; and to all the people of St Mary Magdalene's, Enfield, who managed without me but who have given me so much.

I also wish to express my gratitude to all those who fed and watered me on my travels, especially in North America: Mandy, Michael, Jenny and Katherine Rushby, Patrick and Susan Carter, Paul Grimwood, David and Susan Montgomery, Glenda and David Meakin, and also the Community of Jesus, Cape Cod, Massachusetts. In England, Philip and Monica Spence, Huw and Angela Williams, Jonathan Cox and Stuart Young were hospitable and insightful. For the secrets of cordon bleu cookery in France, I thank Luz Amalia, Guido, Roberto and Matteo Fregonara, and, for food health wisdom, the Community at Stanton House, Oxfordshire, and Sue Woan and Alan Symonds who were there too.

But most of all I thank those who stayed at home: Jessica and Maria, who were left to fend for themselves, and my mother Glenice, who first taught me not only how to prepare food, but also to enjoy it. To them I serve up the menu of this book, with love and gratitude.

CONTENTS

Week Three

Week Four

Week Five

Holy Week

SHROVE TUESDAY

We cannot overemphasize the influence of Jewish tradition on the Christian faith, and nowhere is it more prevalent than in the various rituals and attitudes we have with regard to our food. The central rite of the Christian faith, the Eucharist, owes a tremendous amount to the Passover feast, from which it evolved. Our approach to feasting is hardly a Christian invention and the flipside, the fast, also has origins in Jewish practice. As we embark on a food tourist's journey through Lent, we will surely find ourselves spending time at the tables of both Passover and Holy Communion. We will also find ourselves examining tables today and questioning our relationship with food in this day and age. While climate change often steals the headlines, recent government health warnings against obesity suggest that it is as great a problem, yet at the same time many people strive to obtain the slim figure of a supermodel and eat very little. In obscene contrast, the populations of some nations starve. It is no longer obvious that food is always a blessing, and it is timely to consider food as a multidimensional aspect of today's economical, physical and spiritual life.

Before we begin, it is Shrove Tuesday, the spiritual equivalent of the day before the morning after! This day has different traditions (and titles) associated with it in various parts of the world. In the British Isles, pancakes are the order of the day, made with eggs, flour and milk and served with sugary sauces. They are eaten not just as a final binge before the austerity of Lent kicks in, but also as a way of using up such produce, thereby removing temptation from the ensuing 40 days of fasting, which we call Lent. Other countries have similar traditions: in Iceland, the day is called *Sprengidagur* ('Bursting day') and salted meat and peas are eaten. Meanwhile, the Estonians eat split pea and ham soup on this day. In Sweden, on *Fettisdagen* ('Fat Tuesday') a pastry called *semla* is eaten with hot milk. It is filled with marzipan and whipped cream (and may be eaten on every Tuesday up to Easter). The Finns also eat *semla* but filled with jam instead of marzipan. In Germany and Austria, in Lithuania and in Dutch communities, doughnuts of various kinds are eaten. In Newfoundland there is an added dimension to that of sweet or fatty food: little household objects are hidden in the pancakes (rather as money or trinkets are hidden in British Christmas puddings), and children delight in finding these objects, which are held to bring wealth, love or good fortune.

Shrove Tuesday is not really a feast day as such. It is rather a day prior to a fast day, which is not quite the same thing. Its very name speaks of repentance rather than indulgence and it is good to remember that, while the aroma of maple syrup and pancakes wafts heavenward. 'Shrove' comes from the old English word 'shrive', which means to impose a penance. Thus it was the priest's role to 'shrive' a person: to hear their confession, allocate them penance to amend for their sins and to pronounce God's forgiveness. To be 'shriven' is to have made one's confession and been absolved. The Reformation theologians were rightly concerned about the potential abuses of a mechanistic approach to forgiveness, especially where money changed hands, but it is ironic that Shrove Tuesday is now more associated with gluttony than penitence. Originally, the period from the Sunday before Ash Wednesday (still called 'Quinquagesima' in The Book of Common Prayer) through to the Tuesday was known as 'Shrovetide' and Christians were expected to make confession and receive absolution, in preparation for the great fast of Lent that begins tomorrow.

During that fast, comestibles such as meat, sweet things, fatty food, sauces or anything apparently extravagant would be abandoned until the Easter feast. This tradition is still very much alive, manifesting itself when people give up chocolate or alcohol for Lent. Early tradition also gives us the threefold discipline of prayer (justice towards God), fasting (justice towards self), and almsgiving (justice towards others). The use of the Gloria at the Mass, and Allelluias, were dropped in Lent, and a general feel of austerity was cultivated. Another devotional tradition also developed, in which this very book stands. Early Christian converts went through a process of instruction prior to baptism during the Lent season (in fact, that is how we acquired Lent in the first place). This was a discipline not only of self-denial but of learning, and the idea of reading books for Lent has descended from that desire for knowledge and truth, so that when Easter Day comes we are not only purer but more knowledgeable about the faith we profess and celebrate. St Benedict declared in his Rule that reading and study were important for any monk, but especially in Lent, when each day a book should be read 'straight through'.

It is in the spirit of this tradition that I offer you this volume, not so much to be read straight through but to be tasted daily, rather like a journey around the table of the Bible, or like a 46-course banquet. Each day's 'plate' will complement the others while, I hope, being tasty on its own. Ezekiel was commanded to eat a scroll, to feed on the words of the Lord, as a prophetic action: '[The Lord said] Eat this scroll that I give you and fill your stomach with it. Then I ate it; and in my mouth it was as sweet as honey' (Ezekiel 3:3). In Lent it is good to taste and see the goodness of the Lord, perhaps in a different way, bringing out different or new flavours. This year, try a biblical diet of feasting as well as fasting, in which we shall consider passages that are either obviously or subtly about food or drink, or about the Eucharist, or that point us forward to the heavenly banquet to which our Lord Jesus Christ invites each and every one of us.

So as we fast and feast together this Lent, it remains only for me to wish you *bon appetit*!

JOEL'S FAST

Yet even now, says the Lord, return to me with all your heart, with fasting, with weeping, and with mourning; rend your hearts and not your clothing. Return to the Lord, your God, for he is gracious and merciful, slow to anger, and abounding in steadfast love, and relents from punishing. Who knows whether he will not turn and relent, and leave a blessing behind him, a grain-offering and a drink-offering for the Lord, your God? Blow the trumpet in Zion; sanctify a fast; call a solemn assembly; gather the people. Sanctify the congregation; assemble the aged; gather the children, even infants at the breast. Let the bridegroom leave his room, and the bride her canopy. Between the vestibule and the altar let the priests, the ministers of the Lord, weep. Let them say, 'Spare your people, O Lord, and do not make your heritage a mockery, a byword among the nations.'

JOEL 2:12–17

We saw yesterday how the traditions of Shrovetide have their origins in medieval confession and absolution; there are also similarities to Jewish Passover ritual. As we begin Lent, this passage from Joel is read in many churches today. In his brief work of prophecy, Joel declares the 'day of the Lord', the day on which God appears in a blaze of glory but also heralds drought, famine and anguish (see 1:15–18; 2:1–2). He calls for a widespread and complete manifestation of repentence: fasting, weeping and mourning. The tradition of tearing clothes as a sign of grief is not enough: it is time to tear our hearts and return to the Lord. Everyone—men, women, the old and the young— are to participate in a communal ritual of fasting and prayer that acknowledges guilt and indicates to God their sincerity and love.

If the people did what Joel proposed, it must have been quite a sight. Just imagine the whole of our nation or community united in penitence or sorrow for sin. That would be a real start to Lent, wouldn't it? And it would mark a great contrast with our normal practice: it is hard to get people to come to church on Ash Wednesday, the news media do not mention the significance of the day, and there seems to be just as much sin, pain and grief around as there is on any other day. If people do know about Lent, they do not understand it in the way that Joel understands a general fast. For many, Lent is about 'giving something up', and in this spirit we have created traditions that relate to the spiritual fast of Lent in a physical way. Where there are food traditions for eating up surplus supplies on Shrove Tuesday, there is an inevitable dimension in which we think of future deprivation as inspiring and condoning a little gluttony. It works on a simple level: eat something nice, then deny it to yourself and return to it at the end of the fast, when you will appreciate it all the more. In this way, the spiritual season is physically marked out, but it is very different from what Joel had in mind.

The danger is that the physical dimensions, which are supposed to indicate or underline a spiritual attitude, actually replace it. Lent is not really about 'giving something up'. Giving something up is about Lent. Lent is a period in which we are invited to renew our relationship with God, to 'deny ourselves' and 'take up the cross'. If there is something that comes between us and God, it is good to abandon it in Lent, not only in order to draw closer to God but also to engage in the spiritual discipline of self-denial. There is no point in giving up chocolate, alcohol, sugar, caffeine or some activity if doing so is actually quite easy. Lent is not about what you give up, but about what you do. Sadly, though, over the years, Lent has been perceived negatively as a period for saying 'no', when it is far more challenging and edifying to see it as a period in which we say 'yes' to God as well as 'sorry'. Admittedly, that may involve saying 'no' to ourselves at times.

Fasting is not simply about not eating or giving up certain foods. It is about being humble in the presence of God (Isaiah 58:3–4; Ezra

8:21). The first reference to fasting in the Bible comes when David fasts after his indiscretion with Bathsheba has led to her pregnancy, and he prays that the child may be spared (2 Samuel 12:16). Fasts soon became public events and days of fasting were declared, usually by the elders of the community, although sometimes politics intervened. Jezebel ordered that a fast be observed before the trial of Naboth (1 Kings 21:12), and fasting was considered a good idea before warfare (Judges 20:26; 1 Samuel 7:6; 2 Chronicles 20:3). Fixed fasts were not very common, except that of the Day of Atonement (Yom Kippur), instituted in Leviticus 16:29, which was the fast that hindered Paul's journey to Rome (Acts 27:9). Later, fixed fasts were declared, as in Zechariah 8:19, after the temple was destroyed.

There are two fixed fasts in the Christian calendar. One is today and the other is Good Friday. Flanking Lent for hundreds of years, they are just as useful and relevant today as they ever have been. Many today will receive the imposition of ashes on their foreheads as a mark of penitence—an outward sign of the inward grace of forgiveness granted by God, through the saving work of Christ on the cross, to his faithful people in this faithless and sinful age. Thus it is today that we begin Lent, with humility in our hearts, prayers on our lips and ashes on our heads.

Lord Christ, may we remember that we are dust, and to dust we shall return. Help us turn away from sin to be faithful to you. Amen

SATAN'S TEMPTING OFFER

Then Jesus was led up by the Spirit into the wilderness to be tempted by the devil. He fasted for forty days and forty nights, and afterwards he was famished. The tempter came and said to him, 'If you are the Son of God, command these stones to become loaves of bread.' But he answered, 'It is written, "One does not live by bread alone, but by every word that comes from the mouth of God."'

MATTHEW 4:1–4

We begin with Christ, as we must. Soon we shall be returning to the dinners at the dawn of time, when food laws were set and the tables of time were laid according to the eating plan of creation. We shall return to the sixth day of the world, the very eve of sin, when Adam and Eve ate what they should not have eaten, succumbing to temptation amid the indescribable beauty of the garden of Eden, where permission and prohibition cohabited with eternity in prospect. And that is why we must begin with Christ as we travel through Lent from the genesis of creation to the revelation of the resurrection banquet. We begin with Christ, and we will break fast with him in the resurrection glory of the Easter dawn.

Adam and Eve succumbed. Millennia later, Jesus was tempted in the wilderness and stood firm. Paul summarizes the link between the beginning of the Bible and Jesus' ministry forthrightly:

For since death came through a human being, the resurrection of the dead has also come through a human being; for as all die in Adam, so all will be made alive in Christ… 'The first man, Adam, became a living being'; the

last Adam became a life-giving spirit... The first man was from the earth,
a man of dust; the second man is from heaven.' (1 Corinthians 15:21–22,
45, 47)

Theologically, the connections between Christ and Adam are strong. Adam is tempted by food, symbolizing rebellion and release from the limitations set by the Creator. Jesus, too, is offered and is therefore tempted by the possibility of food in the form of bread. Like Adam, he can fail the test, satisfy his hunger and break free from divine discipline. But Satan has misjudged, for, as the Father and the Son are one (John 14:10–11), Jesus will not divorce his will from that of the Father.

There is an additional ironic twist in that as Christ is the bread of life (John 6:35), Satan tempts him with a caricature of himself. By accepting Satan's advice, Jesus would be turning away from the spiritual to the material. We all need bread but, thanks to God's goodness, we can get it anywhere. There is only one source of mercy and eternal life, however, and that is Christ, the bread of life. Satan is trying to get Jesus to abandon his mission at the first hurdle.

Jesus does not succeed merely because he can conquer hunger. Turning stones into bread is a simple miracle, comparable perhaps to changing water into wine (John 2:1–11). For many, Christ's 40 days in the wilderness are an inspiration to an ascetic life, or a period of prayer and fasting. The discipline of such fasting, whether in a monastery or a maisonette, has many advantages: fasting is rarely bad for you (and if it is, you should not do it). Today's secular equivalent, the 'detox', has physical benefits comparable with the spiritual benefits of fasting. To combine the two approaches is thoroughly commendable, not least because it restores the connection between body and spirit that life today seems to separate, and reminds us that our relationship with God is about body and soul, unified in prayerful action. This is what Jesus shows us by resisting the first temptation. Turning down stonegrain bread is not about hunger; it is about relationship with God, manifest in the living Word of the bread of life. Defeating the pangs of hunger is not an end in itself but a means to greater holiness and a deeper relationship with God.

In resisting Satan, Christ undoes the damage that Adam did, restoring fallen humanity, healing the wound of sin. But his victory over Satan does not mean that we are not tempted. Whether we are thinking trivially of cream cakes ('naughty but nice') or seriously of things that hinder our relationship with God, temptation is ever present. Indeed, it is probably more of a problem now than in Jesus' time, because there is far more by which to be tempted. Fortunately, while the temptations are greater than they were, the stakes of sin have been significantly reduced by Christ, whose own resistance to temptation not only shows us the way to salvation but is the first act in his divine task of clearing the path that takes us to the forgiving Father, reigning on the throne of grace.

Father God, we are your children, negligent of your love. Give us a spirit of fasting this Lent, that we may be reconnected to you in renewal and restoration of body and soul. Amen

ADAM'S NEW WORLD

Then God said, 'Let us make humankind in our image, according to our likeness; and let them have dominion over the fish of the sea, and over the birds of the air, and over the cattle, and over all the wild animals of the earth, and over every creeping thing that creeps upon the earth.' So God created humankind in his image, in the image of God he created them; male and female he created them. God blessed them, and God said to them, 'Be fruitful and multiply, and fill the earth and subdue it; and have dominion over the fish of the sea and over the birds of the air and over every living thing that moves upon the earth.'

GENESIS 1:26–28

The Bible has a lot to answer for. This famous passage, in which humankind makes a first domineering appearance, lies not only at the root of Judeo-Christian attitudes to our environment (which have tended to be negative) but also at the heart of secular and atheistic conceptions of the meaning of life. It has been consistently misunderstood by both faithful and faithless generations. John Gray, a London professor of European Thought, writes, 'Marxists and free-market economists never tire of ridiculing the idea that other living things have intrinsic value. In their view, other species are just means to the satisfaction of human wants and the earth itself is a site for the realization of human ambitions.'[1] This opinion is striking in two ways.

Firstly, the idea that all creation is ours, and that our dominion amounts to divinely ordained domination of our environment, has been retained by those who have lost almost every other aspect of faith. Even where faith in God has gone, faith in ourselves is as strong as ever. Yet the idea that we are the monarchs of the natural world makes little sense where there is no doctrine of a Creator who made us so. For Christians, our uniqueness in creation is easily explained in today's passage, for we, unlike any other creature, are created 'in the image of God'. So there is a distinctive kind of nonsense in an atheistic worldview that places humanity at the pinnacle of creation.

Worse still, there is then no ethical basis on which to assert any human right of dominion or domination, nor any being to whom we might be answerable for the way in which we treat other creatures. No theory of evolution, biology, cosmology or secular humanism can give any account as to why humans can consider themselves 'in charge'. At best, these worldviews offer the idea that because we are in control, we must, in some sense, have a right to be. But, as the 18th-century philosopher David Hume put it, 'an "is" does not make an "ought"'—that is, because something is the case, it does not follow that it ought to be so.

Secondly, the view that dominion amounts to domination is not held by the majority of Christians, nor should it be. Some people believe that secularists have pinched from Christianity the idea that the world is a playground for humans, but this is a misrepresentation of our faith. The fact that Christians nowadays may sometimes be involved in animal cruelty, intensive farming, laboratory testing or other unpleasant or morally dubious modes of stewardship does not mean that Christianity, or God, advocates such behaviour. Some Christians steal but that does not mean that Christ advocates theft.

Like atheists, Christians live in a world damaged by sin. The opening passages of Genesis establish the first humans as monarchs of their world, put into Eden to manage the creatures over whom they have power and for whom they must take responsibility. The proper attitude towards fellow creatures is therefore not one of domination, abuse or exploitation. Reverence, care, responsibility and mutuality are the attitudes that should and often do characterize the relationship between humans and other creatures. Sadly, however, the biblical idea of 'dominion' has always been abused and still is.

Ironically, the kind of view that John Gray criticizes as a relic of theism—that dominion equals domination—is itself a form of atheism, for anyone who believes this is in fact denouncing or denying the will of the Creator. As we shall see as we proceed through the Bible, it is not true that God gave humans animals as toys; rather that our interdependence is itself a fundamental part of the created order. To deny that is to deny God. We might expect such a denial from atheists but should be surprised to find it among the faithful, for when it comes to our relationship with other creatures, it is a matter of faith, even for those who profess to have none. Ultimately, the ways in which we steward the resources of the earth reflect what we hold true and dear about the world in which we live, how it came to be and where it will all end up.

Lord Jesus, forgive us when we think too highly of ourselves and thereby write you out of the equation of life. Reveal yourself to those who appreciate your world but do not see you in it, so that all may be brought to the glorious redemption of the children of God. Amen

ADAM'S APPLE

Now the serpent was more crafty than any other wild animal that the Lord God had made. He said to the woman, 'Did God say, "You shall not eat from any tree in the garden"?' The woman said to the serpent, 'We may eat of the fruit of the trees in the garden; but God said, "You shall not eat of the fruit of the tree that is in the middle of the garden, nor shall you touch it, or you shall die."' But the serpent said to the woman, 'You will not die; for God knows that when you eat of it your eyes will be opened, and you will be like God, knowing good and evil.' So when the woman saw that the tree was good for food, and that it was a delight to the eyes, and that the tree was to be desired to make one wise, she took of its fruit and ate; and she also gave some to her husband, who was with her, and he ate.

GENESIS 3:1–6

Many people think this text is all about sin: it is about not doing what you are told, breaking rules, disobeying God. They are not wrong, but this passage is also about food. It is about what to eat and what not to eat. We take it for granted that God the Creator has the right to tell the man and the woman what they should eat, but, in our supermarket age, this is not something that many are willing to endure. From a very early age we begin to make and express food preferences and to resent being told what to eat by parents or others in authority. Parents know that to give in to the food preferences expressed by toddlers is to make a rod for their own backs, as fussy eaters can grow, sometimes at a frightening rate, into adults who may lack self-discipline, wisdom or intelligence when it comes to shopping, cooking and dining. There is something fundamentally childish about this man's and this woman's attitude and desire—a mixture of knowing what is right and wrong but also wanting to rebel, to seize power and discover whether the consequences are as dire as the parent figure tells them.

There is a sense in which nothing changes. Parents know best but children want to assert their own independence. It is exactly the same when it comes to our relationship with our heavenly Father, who, having created us, knows what is best for us. Yet we want to go our own way, assert our own will and enjoy what we take to be freedom to do as we please.

Nowadays, food independence is probably more dangerous than it ever has been. For Adam and Eve there was only one plant—the tree of the knowledge of good and evil—that they were forbidden to touch, and they were forbidden its fruit because it was bad for them. Today we have so much more choice, more to tempt us and more to hurt us. And because it is available, we succumb to indiscipline and indulge in foods that are distinctly bad for us. Either the foodstuffs themselves are dangerous, such as the Japanese fish *fugu*, which if not prepared properly can be lethal, or the additives we use in cookery are potentially dangerous, such as propyl gallate, butylated hydroxyanisole (BHA) and butylated hydroxytoluene (BHT), which may be added to oil but can cause cancer. The ubiquitous monosodium glutamate (MSG) is a chemical that many believe can enhance the flavour of food but can also be harmful.

The other danger from foodstuffs concerns the quantities we consume. With so much food available to us, it is easy to be disobedient to our bodies' needs: to consume more than we can or should take in, and therefore cause harm to ourselves. Overeating used to be considered a weakness of character—to be ridiculed, perhaps—but now it is reaching epidemic proportions in the West and is more like a sociological and physical disease. Yet overeating is a form of disobedience to nature—a rejection of our natural limitations and the spiritual dimension of our physical lives. This disobedience was classically articulated in the tradition of the 'Seven Deadly Sins', of which gluttony is one. Today, gluttony is perhaps more dangerous than ever before, particularly now that increased availability of food has produced the twofold problem of foodstuffs addictions and 'comfort' eating.

There are two levels at which overeating and dangerous eating are selfish. Firstly, those who hurt themselves in any way cause financial, emotional and physical stress to the families, societies and communities to which they belong. Increasing trends in obesity are going to cost Western governments a fortune in the coming years, drawing funds from other conditions that may cause suffering to those who cannot be said to be so responsible for the diseases they endure.

Secondly, wilfully doing anything that endangers our own health is tantamount to a rejection of our status as created beings, into whom God has breathed spiritual and physical life. Those who take risks with what they eat could be indicating that they do not value the life with which they have been blessed. They may also believe that pleasure is a driving dimension of existence. The life we have is not given us solely for our own benefit, and it is not therefore entirely ours to dispose of or abuse. Undisciplined eating is a form of slow suicide, and we are as accountable to God for what we eat as for anything else that we do to ourselves or others.

Lord, help us turn away from sin and death to the freedom found in obedience to your word of life. Amen

WEEK ONE

CAIN AND ABEL'S FAMILY FEUD

Eve… bore Cain, saying, 'I have produced a man with the help of the Lord.' Next she bore his brother Abel. Now Abel was a keeper of sheep, and Cain a tiller of the ground… Cain brought to the Lord an offering of the fruit of the ground, and Abel for his part brought of the firstlings of his flock, their fat portions. And the Lord had regard for Abel and his offering, but for Cain and his offering he had no regard. So Cain was very angry, and his countenance fell. The Lord said to Cain, 'Why are you angry, and why has your countenance fallen? If you do well, will you not be accepted? And if you do not do well, sin is lurking at the door; its desire is for you, but you must master it.' Cain said to his brother Abel, 'Let us go out to the field.' And when they were in the field, Cain rose up against his brother Abel and killed him. Then the Lord said to Cain, 'Where is your brother Abel?' He said, 'I do not know; am I my brother's keeper?' And the Lord said, 'What have you done? Listen; your brother's blood is crying out to me from the ground! And now you are cursed… When you till the ground, it will no longer yield to you its strength; you will be a fugitive and a wanderer on the earth.'

GENESIS 4:1–12 (ABRIDGED)

There is an old saying that seems very relevant today: 'The family that eats together stays together.' In 2007, UNICEF published a report about the quality of life for young people, and the apparent lack of 'happiness' among British children put them at the bottom of the list.[2] While we should be cautious of statistics that try to measure well-being, UNICEF is a highly reputable United Nations organization. Researchers found that only 60 per cent of children spoke to their parents regularly and a third did not eat meals with them. There does, then, seem to be some truth in the old adage.

Yet, when families gather for meals there can be trouble, and not only over what is eaten and in what quantity ('Eat your greens, dear'). Confrontations occur at meal times that can damage the fabric of families. Where different generations do eat together, that could well be the only thing that they do together, which increases the potential for conflict during the meal. This is precisely why some people find Christmas so stressful, for it brings together a group of people who are not usually together, who are not accustomed to sharing space, resources, opinions or feelings, and their seemingly enforced proximity can be a recipe for disaster.

It is a shame that the dining table is not always the place of heavenly banqueting and familial harmony. It need not be a war zone, of course, and in many contexts it is not. I hope that you, like me, have happy memories of meals shared with family and friends, whether they be Sunday lunches, evening dinner parties or seasonal or wedding celebrations. Cathy Campbell, a Canadian priest, reminds us:

Food is at the heart of human culture. It is a part of all our lives. We each eat every day, and hopefully more than once a day. It is part of our material life as day six creatures, yet it also opens us to the Sacred… Our food ways reflect our relationships: with the earth, with each other, and with God.[3]

This is why the story of Cain and Abel is so sad and so troubling.

On one level, the two sons of Adam and Eve are archetypes: Cain is the arable farmer and Abel the shepherd, and between them they reflect two forms of stewardship. We are told that the Lord does not have equal regard for the fruit of their labours, and jealousy overcomes Cain, even though God warns him of the risk. Like his father before him, Cain fails a test, oversteps the limits, lets sin in, distances himself, denies responsibility and so is cast out of favour. Cain is a bad farmer in both senses of the word 'bad'. Conversely, his brother, with whom he does not see himself as being in any meaningful relationship ('Am I my brother's keeper?'), is a good shepherd. Cain resents the success, productivity and divine acceptance of his brother's pastoral gifts, so plans and executes his murder. It is all vaguely familiar and the similarities between Abel and Christ are striking. As we saw yesterday, Christ undoes the sin of Adam, but he also has to deal with Cain and all who follow him in the paths of malevolence and murder.

Christ, good shepherd, who laid down your life for us, restore table fellowship to our fractured society until that day when your whole family dines together in your eternal kingdom. Amen

NOAH SAVES THE ANIMALS

And every animal, every creeping thing, and every bird, everything that moves on the earth, went out of the ark by families. Then Noah built an altar to the Lord, and took of every clean animal and of every clean bird, and offered burnt-offerings on the altar. And when the Lord smelt the pleasing odour, the Lord said in his heart, 'I will never again curse the ground because of humankind, for the inclination of the human heart is evil from youth; nor will I ever again destroy every living creature as I have done... The fear and dread of you shall rest on every animal of the earth, and on every bird of the air, on everything that creeps on the ground, and on all the fish of the sea; into your hand they are delivered. Every moving thing that lives shall be food for you; and just as I gave you the green plants, I give you everything.

GENESIS 8:19–21; 9:2–3

If a figure from Genesis can be a saint, Noah is the patron of animal welfare. He does what God tells him, building an ark and saving wildlife from extinction. He shares his living space with and provides for those who are utterly dependent upon the arrangements that he and his family have made. Yet, as soon the flood is over, Noah takes some of his flock, killing and cooking them in sacrifice to God, who promises in return never to hurt creation in this way again. This part of the story reflects a very clear line of power and authority: God is in charge and we do what he says, but God has put us in charge of animals so they must bow to our needs and desires. After the flood, the status quo created in Adam's time is well and truly restored.

Biblical as this logic is, it seems a little harsh. In so many senses, we have moved on a long way since Noah and can contemplate approaches of which he could never have conceived, such as factory farming, genetic modification, cloning, and breeding for human organ transplants. As Dr Mike Appleby puts it, 'Noah is sailing the ark of society into the twenty-first century above the flood of human population growth, technological change and environmental damage. Animals are on board, and we need to look after them.'[4]

Animal welfare is an ancient and topical issue. Whether we are talking of the conditions under which chickens live and eggs are laid, or the use of mice, monkeys or rabbits for medical or other tests, many people have strong views on the subject. In the 1990s, the British government asked Professor Michael Banner to chair a committee to consider the ethical implications of certain breeding techniques for farm animals. Professor Banner is a Christian theologian and one of the conclusions his group reached was that there are certain kinds or levels of harm that should never be inflicted upon animals. Where harm is not prohibited, it should be justified such that the benefit (to humankind or other animals) of the harm outweighs the suffering caused, but nevertheless harm should be minimized.[5] We can hardly disagree with these recommendations, although some people would want to go further in banning experimentation upon or manipulation of animals.

The Banner Committee recommended that a commission be set up as a kind of 'ethical watchdog' to look at issues in animal welfare in the UK. The proposal was rejected but the need for vigilance, especially in the light of emerging technologies, has not gone away. Noah teaches us that even if the ultimate goal of our animal husbandry is to eat them, we should still look after them under the best conditions we can manage. The ark provided a refuge for humans and other animals alike, and, while our Jewish ancestors saw animals as lower than humanity and therefore implied that to a large extent animals were saved for our benefit, we know from our reading of the Gospels that there is a divine love for all creation: 'Look at the birds of the air; they neither sow nor reap nor gather into barns, and yet your heavenly

Father feeds them. Are you not of more value than they?' (Matthew 6:26).

We are in the same boat together, perhaps even more so than when humans and animals sailed in the ark together millennia ago. Conservationists may tell us that the extinction of a species is not good for the species itself or for us, or for the environment we share—our fragile ecosystem on precarious planet earth. There is also something in our nature that laments such extinction. And that lamentation may have something to do with having been created in the image of God, so that we, like God, deplore the loss of any part of creation.

O Lord, we pray for all who care for the animals who live and die for our needs and desires. May we, with them, remember your love for all creation and the hope of eternal life brought about in Jesus Christ our Lord. Amen

NOAH GETS DRUNK

Noah, a man of the soil, was the first to plant a vineyard. He drank some of the wine and became drunk, and he lay uncovered in his tent. And Ham, the father of Canaan, saw the nakedness of his father, and told his two brothers outside. Then Shem and Japheth took a garment, laid it on both their shoulders, and walked backwards and covered the nakedness of their father; their faces were turned away, and they did not see their father's nakedness. When Noah awoke from his wine and knew what his youngest son had done to him, he said, 'Cursed be Canaan; lowest of slaves shall he be to his brothers.' ... All the days of Noah were nine hundred and fifty years; and he died.

GENESIS 9:20–25, 29

The French Protestant reformer John Calvin (1509–64) claimed that 'wine is God's special drink. The purpose of good wine is to inspire us to a livelier sense of gratitude to God'.⁶ Nevertheless, Noah's story reminds us of the dangers and consequences of too much alcohol. The book of Proverbs has some good advice in that the writer acknowledges the dangers of being led astray by drink (20:1) and instructs leaders to avoid it (31:4), yet strong drink is good for healing: 'Give strong drink to one who is perishing, and wine to those in bitter distress' (v. 6). The good Samaritan follows this advice when he pours wine on the wounds of the robbed traveller (Luke 10:34). Paul cautions his readers against drunkeness: 'Do not get drunk with wine, for that is debauchery; but be filled with the Spirit' (Ephesians 5:18). Biblical authors knew about wine from experience and observation, and show us that the social problems associated with overindulgence were very similar to those of today.

As Noah so vividly demonstrated, alcohol has an effect on body and mind that varies according to the amount consumed. Various drinks have different strengths, thereby accelerating the impact of the drug in the bloodstream. Tolerance varies, too, such that it is hard to say how strong Noah's drink was. We do not know whether he was 'used to his drink' or whether he got drunk the first time he tried his new concoction. We can assume, however, that, like almost all alcoholic drink since, Noah's brew involved ethanol, an organic compound, easily soluble, made up of carbon, oxygen and hydrogen. When consumed, it passes quickly through the stomach into the intestines, where absorption into the blood takes place, having an almost immediate effect on the central nervous system and leading to a series of symptoms of poisoning. Initially, inhibitions are lowered (which may account for Noah's nakedness) but, as the concentration of alcohol in the blood increases, the ability to respond to stimuli decreases significantly (hence legal bans on drinking and driving or operating machinery). Speech may become slurred and balance affected. If blood-alcohol reaches a very high concentration (greater than 0.35 grammes per 100 millilitres of blood), a coma may be induced and death may result.

Alcohol is a fast-acting drug that poisons the blood and inhibits the nervous system. Fortunately for those who enjoy its taste and effects, our bodies are built to deal with it (through the liver) but too much causes hangovers and disease. Some people suffer from alcoholism, a recognized medical condition of addiction and dependency, which may be caused not only by consistent abuse of alcohol but also by a genetic predisposition to addiction. It is very important to distinguish between someone who drinks heavily and an alcoholic, for alcoholism can be triggered or reactivated by only a small amount of alcohol and some heavy drinkers are not alcoholics in that they are not actually dependent upon the substance. There is no evidence that the Bible recognizes this distinction: most warnings and prohibitions in the Bible imply heavy drinking and caution against it.

Noah, then, was a heavy drinker on at least one occasion. The story does not say that he learnt his lesson, although he did live to a great age. Indeed, it is often suggested that a modest amount of alcohol can be good for health. His story is not simply about wine but about its effects, for he becomes angry and curses his grandson Canaan, making him subservient to his brothers. It was a cruel and vengeful act, which not only led to later justification for Israel's enslavement and disparagement of the Canaanites, but also served, some argue, as a basis for slavery in America. It is clear not only that alcohol is a substance to be treated with respect and care but also that the consequences of consumption are a cause for concern. Drinking alcohol is not a sin in itself but it can lead to sin, and a drunk person is to be held responsible for their actions while under the influence. While they may not have been in control of themselves when drunk, getting drunk is something for which Noah, and all who follow him, will be called to account before God, whose primary intention in giving us wine is to ' gladden the human heart' (Psalm 104:15).

Father, you bless us with the wine of your kingdom, poured out as Christ's blood. Help us to respect its power and live always as witnesses to your love and mercy revealed in the same Jesus Christ our Lord. Amen

ABRAHAM'S GUESTS

The Lord appeared to Abraham by the oaks of Mamre... in the heat of the day. He looked up and saw three men standing near him... he ran from the tent entrance to meet them, and bowed down to the ground. He said, 'My lord, if I find favour with you, do not pass by your servant. Let a little water be brought, and wash your feet, and rest yourselves under the tree. Let me bring a little bread, that you may refresh yourselves, and after that you may pass on—since you have come to your servant.' So they said, 'Do as you have said.' And Abraham hastened into the tent to Sarah, and said, 'Make ready quickly three measures of choice flour, knead it, and make cakes.' Abraham ran to the herd, and took a calf, tender and good, and gave it to the servant, who hastened to prepare it. Then he took curds and milk and the calf that he had prepared, and set it before them; and he stood by them under the tree while they ate.

GENESIS 18:1–8 (ABRIDGED)

This story served as the inspiration for a very famous icon painted by Sergei Rublev (1370–1430) for the Cathedral of the Trinity at Sergius Lavra in Russia. Rublev's masterpiece expresses the trinitarian nature of God, transcending a simple portrayal of the men who visit Abraham for a late lunch, drawing on the tradition that the three were angels, representing God as Father, Son and Holy Spirit.

Whether the story prefigures the doctrine of the Trinity or not, it is clearly about hospitality. Abraham's welcome is a typically bedouin one. He bows in greeting and implies that it would be a discourtesy if they were to decline his offer of refreshment. The offer to wash their feet reminds us of Jesus washing the disciples' feet at the last supper

(John 13:5–12), but it was also a common courtesy, which, when Jesus entered the house of Simon, was denied to him: 'Do you see this woman? I entered your house; you gave me no water for my feet, but she has bathed my feet with her tears and dried them with her hair… You did not anoint my head with oil, but she has anointed my feet with ointment' (Luke 7:44, 46). It is still true: a friend of mine visiting Sudan recently described how, on arriving at a house, he was immediately attended to in this way. He was deeply moved, recalling Christ's footwashing. Yet what for us typifies service and humility was, and still is in some places, a hospitable but standard act of welcome.

Writing in 1959, the intrepid Englishman Wilfred Thesiger described a meeting in the Arabian desert that resonates with Abraham's encounter:

Coming across the sands were three Arabs… We greeted them, asked the news, made coffee… dished up the hare and the bread and set it before them… saying… that they were our guests. They asked us to join them but we refused, repeating that they were our guests… When they had finished bin Kabina put a sticky lump of dates in a dish and called us over to feed.[7]

They gave their meal to the guests, and therefore had little to eat themselves. It may have been so for Abraham, who insisted on feeding his three guests with freshly killed meat and homemade cakes. His generosity must have endured for a while: killing a calf, preparing, cooking, serving and eating it must have taken a long time. And then, like those in Thesiger's story, Abraham stood waiting while the angelic strangers ate. He served them but did not presume to recline and eat with them. His actions remind us of words from Hebrews 13:2: 'Do not neglect to show hospitality to strangers, for by doing that some have entertained angels without knowing it.' Jesus himself suggests that hospitality is an ancient principle of faith: 'I was hungry and you gave me food, I was thirsty and you gave me something to drink, I was a stranger and you welcomed me' (Matthew 25:35).

If a stranger visited your house, would you prepare a roast meal and bake cakes on the spot? You probably wouldn't, not because you are not generous but because, in Western culture, it is not normal. But you would probably offer a drink and some readily available snack. If it were a meal time, you might invite them to join you, sharing what you have. As a clergyman I am often on the receiving end of such generosity, which has become enshrined in that archetypal phrase, 'More tea, Vicar?' There is something distinctively human about our tendency to share companionship and food simultaneously. It is tempting to wonder whether it is in some way a mark of our having been made in the image of God. In Christ, he shows us a hospitality and generosity that draw us through his own offering of himself to a welcome at the heavenly banquet, of which Abraham's encounter at Mamre may indeed be a brief, trinitarian foretaste.

Generous God, give us grace to be hospitable to friend and stranger alike, that they, with us, may rest in your presence and dine on the love you reveal to us as Father, Son and Holy Spirit. Amen

---

JACOB'S SOUP

There were twins in [Rebekah's] womb. The first came out red, all his body like a hairy mantle; so they named him Esau. Afterwards his brother came out, with his hand gripping Esau's heel; so he was named Jacob... When the boys grew up, Esau was a skilful hunter, a man of the field, while Jacob was a quiet man, living in tents. Isaac loved Esau, because he was fond of game; but Rebekah loved Jacob. Once when Jacob was cooking a stew, Esau came in from the field, and he was famished. Esau said to Jacob, 'Let me eat some of that red stuff, for I am famished!' ... Jacob said, 'First sell me your birthright.' Esau said, 'I am about to die; of what use is a birthright to me?' Jacob said, 'Swear to me first.' So he swore to him, and sold his birthright to Jacob. Then Jacob gave Esau bread and lentil stew, and he ate and drank, and rose and went his way. Thus Esau despised his birthright.

GENESIS 25:24–31 (ABRIDGED)

I am not a great fan of lentils, but if you would like to try what Jacob served Esau (for a significantly lesser cost), this is how you do it. Take 2 cups of split red lentils, 8 cups of vegetable stock, a large onion, a leek, 3 sticks of celery and 2 carrots, cut them up and simmer for about half an hour. The lentils should disintegrate. You may need to add a little water as it cooks, but remember, this is stew, not soup. Towards the end of cooking, add a teaspoonful of ground cumin and a good slosh of white wine vinegar. Meanwhile, fry another onion in olive oil until it caramelises and add it to the stew. In Old Testament times, stews were the most common cooked meal and people would dip bread into them. I doubt that Jacob

36

knew about croutons, but you could use them instead.

The distinction between a soup and a stew is a fine one but, when it comes to Jacob's dish, the King James Bible uses the evocative phrase 'mess of pottage'—and 'pottage' still describes an uneven deal in which something valuable is obtained in return for something relatively trivial. Esau's protestation that his birthright was worthless if he was starving is not very convincing, and we can imagine that what began as a bit of banter turned serious when Jacob realized he had an opportunity to put one over his slightly elder brother. On the other hand, it is hard for us, who can so easily buy any number of readymade soups or other meals at the supermarket, to appreciate what it is to starve or what Esau's birthright was really worth.

Esau was a hunter, although he is not the first hunter named in the Bible. That honour goes to Nimrod (Genesis 10:8–9). Hunting was no easy game and Esau could well have spent days roaming, tracking, chasing and failing to catch (probably) wild gazelle. Gazelles were sometimes killed on the hoof but could also be captured and brought home for rearing. Esau might also have been hunting birds such as quail, pheasant or peacocks. He and his father Isaac were lovers of game; Jacob, at this stage, is serving vegetarian food, although later in life (as we shall see tomorrow) he became a shepherd for his uncle Laban.

Nevertheless, Esau comes home empty-handed and hungry, and the cycle of deceit begins. Jacob cons Esau out of his birthright and later adds insult to injury by pretending to be Esau in order to gain his father's blessing (27:15–38). Again food plays a major part in this deception and, as my grandfather used to say, 'there's no robbing bellies'. Like a meal eaten, the deed is done: Jacob has secured for himself a double share of the inheritance and the rightful headship of the family, which had been Esau's birthright. When Isaac realizes he has been deceived, he can do nothing: an oral blessing was legally binding just as a verbal undertaking can be today. Jacob's mother Rebekah then facilitates his escape from the wrath of twice-deceived Esau (vv. 41–45).

When Jacob wants to work for his uncle Laban, also an expert in manipulating others, Laban makes Jacob work for seven years for the hand of Rachel. Laban, however, dresses Leah as Rachel, thus turning the tables on the trick that Jacob and Rebekah played on Isaac and Esau. Laban then makes Jacob work for another seven years to get Rachel, the one whom he loved all along (29:1–28).

Jacob began his career by using food to manipulate his brother and father. As we shall see tomorrow, he went on to attempt genetic manipulation in order to increase his wealth and feed what was to become a very large family.

Lord, hear those who cry to you in hunger. Nourish them and protect them from all who would exploit their need, for the sake of Jesus Christ, the bread of life. Amen

JACOB'S SHEEP

[Jacob said to Laban] 'Let me pass through all your flock today, removing from it every speckled and spotted sheep and every black lamb, and the spotted and speckled among the goats; and such shall be my wages... Then Jacob took fresh rods of poplar and almond and plane, and peeled white streaks in them, exposing the white of the rods. He set the rods that he had peeled in front of the flocks in the troughs... And since they bred when they came to drink, the flocks bred in front of the rods, and so the flocks produced young that were striped, speckled, and spotted. Jacob separated the lambs, and set the faces of the flocks toward the striped and the completely black animals in the flock of Laban; and he put his own droves apart, and did not put them with Laban's flock. Whenever the stronger of the flock were breeding, Jacob laid the rods in the troughs before the eyes of the flock, that they might breed among the rods, but for the feebler of the flock he did not lay them there; so the feebler were Laban's, and the stronger Jacob's.

GENESIS 30:32, 37–42

This Genesis story about genetic engineering reveals how primitive and misinformed early attempts at selective breeding were. It was not until the Augustinian monk Gregor Mendel (1822–64) revealed the hidden details of genetics that understanding of chromosomes and family resemblance became commonplace. Now we take it for granted that ginger hair (like Esau's) is caused by a recessive gene, but Jacob had no idea of this.

Nowadays genetic engineering is a much more serious and successful enterprise. Animals are modified in order to grow faster (pigs and chickens) or to be disease-resistant (cattle), for pharma-ceutical products (genetically modified sheep's milk can be used to treat emphysema), for organ transplants (from pigs to humans), for treating cancer (mice) or to increase our scientific knowledge (cloned sheep). For better or worse, there are reasons for and outcomes from this science, the rights and wrongs of which are still very much under debate. It may be very easy to criticize these ventures on the grounds that God did not create animals to be tampered with by humankind and that for us to do so is to turn dominion into domination or even abuse, but a cursory reading of the story of Jacob's sheep reveals that that is precisely what he tried to do. Would Jacob have used better technology had it been available to him?

Jacob kept sheep for two reasons—to produce clothes and food—just as we do today. Like Jacob, modern farmers seek to get the best yield from flocks, which would not exist in the first place were they not being stewarded for meat, milk and wool. When we bring animals into the world (whether we 'modify' them or not), we have a God-given responsibility for their welfare. With all due respect to vegetarians, this does not mean that we cannot eat them, especially if that is the main reason why they are being farmed. If we put aside the perspective that says 'If I were a lamb I would not like to be killed', it is easier to see how our responsibilities lie in taking care of how animals live and die, rather than if they live and die. Whether we should farm livestock and how we should farm livestock are different issues, and, given that we do farm livestock, we should be very concerned with how we do so. That is why the Banner Committee concluded as it did (see 'Noah saves the animals', p. 28).

On the other hand, you may feel that Jacob was a devious and manipulative person and we should not pay too much attention to his sheep. If you take the view that he is not someone whose actions are praiseworthy, then it may follow that his attempt to pervert the course of nature with spotted and striped bits of wood is as wrong as it is pathetic. You may also feel the same about those who 'play God' today. Nevertheless, it is true that some genetically modified animals suffer welfare disadvantages and others do not. The pigs that were bred to grow faster at Beltsville, USA, in the mid 1980s developed severe arthritis, and their human-inflicted suffering was deplorable. Fortunately, lessons have been learned: breeding in this way is more regulated and there is a general agreement that such suffering is unacceptable. Similarly, mice that are bred to be susceptible to cancers also suffer, but in the cause of the alleviation of human suffering. While hurting animals in order to develop the latest perfume is almost universally frowned upon, onco-mice (as they are called) challenge our sensitivities in a more complex way.

Sometimes our reading of the Bible raises more questions than it yields answers. What do you feel and think about Jacob's sheep and their genetically modified descendants?

Heavenly Father, your care for your world is infinite and beyond our comprehension. Amid the complexities of life today, help us be holy stewards of the mysteries of your creation. Amen

JOSEPH'S STOREHOUSES

[Joseph] gathered up all the food of the seven years when there was plenty in the land of Egypt, and stored up food in the cities; he stored up in every city the food from the fields around it. So Joseph stored up grain in such abundance—like the sand of the sea—that he stopped measuring it; it was beyond measure... The seven years of plenty that prevailed in the land of Egypt came to an end; and the seven years of famine began to come, just as Joseph had said. There was famine in every country, but throughout the land of Egypt there was bread. When all the land of Egypt was famished, the people cried to Pharaoh for bread. Pharaoh said to all the Egyptians, 'Go to Joseph; what he says to you, do.' And since the famine had spread over all the land, Joseph opened all the storehouses, and sold to the Egyptians, for the famine was severe in the land of Egypt. Moreover, all the world came to Joseph in Egypt to buy grain, because the famine became severe throughout the world.

GENESIS 41:48–49, 53–57

While the story of Joseph is straightforward and well-known, relating it to known Egyptian history is complex and contentious. Ahmed Osman claimed that Joseph was the 18th-dynasty (c.1570–1352BC) Vizier Seph, whose name is a shortening of Yu-Seph or Osarseph. In the first century AD, Josephus quoted a 400-year-old history of the Egyptian priest Manetho, stating that in the time of Amenhotep III, Osarseph ('Vizier Seph') forbade the worship of the Egyptian gods. This Seph, who is also referred to as Yuya, apparently had very similar titles conferred on him to those listed for Joseph in Genesis and married a high-ranking priest's daughter called Tuya, also known as Asenath: 'Thus Joseph gained authority over the land of Egypt' (Genesis 41:45). Yuya was the father-in-law of the Pharaoh Amenhotep III, who ruled from 1417 to 1379BC. The tombs of Tuya and Yuya have been discovered in the Valley of the Kings near Luxor.[8]

Another theory suggests that Joseph was the famous but mysterious Egyptian architect Imhotep, who designed the first pyramid at Sakkara. While this is unlikely, the Sakkara site, easily visited today, contains some very large grain storage areas dug into the ground but open to the sky. We need not assume that Joseph was Imhotep and that he built these structures, but they are fascinating archeological evidence for large-scale grain storage in ancient Egypt. As a system of chambers they are far too big to be tombs, and they could have stored vast amounts of grain, perhaps collected during years of plenty, to be sold and distributed during leaner times.[9]

The consensus of scholarly opinion rejects any strong correlation between the biblical Joseph and known Egyptological archaeology and history, but this is not to say that we should treat Joseph as a fictional or archetypal character. Indeed, Genesis may be as historically reliable as any source. If events happened more or less as related therein, we must admire Joseph for his perspicacity and tenacity, and consider him to be both an economic and a spiritual visionary. Joseph saved thousands of lives by inventing and administering a policy that survives in our world of commerce and banking. If you produce more than you need, save it, and if others are lacking, share what you have (albeit at a price). Pension schemes today work in a similar way: put aside what you have while you can afford it so that when you have nothing, you will have something—enough to live on, you hope. In recent years, some pension schemes have truly messed up this principle, either by failing to invest sufficiently or by plundering reserves at the wrong time for the wrong purposes. It is rather ironic that Joseph succeeded all those years ago while major companies get it wrong today.

Meanwhile, progress has been made where famine is concerned. The UN says that there were 540 million malnourished people in

1979–81 and 580 million in 1989–1990. World population increased by 23 per cent in the intervening period, which means that the proportion of starving people actually declined. Today, 90 per cent of all people receive enough food, while 90 per cent of those who do not are still getting 90 per cent of the calories they need. The problem is not lack of food but its distribution, which is often controlled by unjust, incompetent or corrupt governments.

I am sure that, like me, you give money to charities that alleviate world hunger. It is not a lost cause and, as the recent *Make Poverty History* campaign indicates, it is not an impossible goal. Joseph made famine history in his time and, if someone today can galvanize opinion and practice as he did, then the starving stand a chance.

Lord, you have given us the vision and the power to feed the hungry and help the needy. Give us the will to persevere, for the sake of Jesus Christ, the friend of the poor and Prince of Peace. Amen

WEEK TWO

MOSES' FAST FOOD

The Lord said to Moses and Aaron in the land of Egypt: … Tell the whole congregation of Israel that on the tenth of this month they are to take a lamb for each family, a lamb for each household. If a household is too small for a whole lamb, it shall join its closest neighbour in obtaining one; the lamb shall be divided in proportion to the number of people who eat of it. Your lamb shall be without blemish, a year-old male; you may take it from the sheep or from the goats. You shall keep it until the fourteenth day of this month; then the whole assembled congregation of Israel shall slaughter it at twilight. They shall take some of the blood and put it on the two doorposts and the lintel of the houses in which they eat it. They shall eat the lamb that same night; they shall eat it roasted over the fire with unleavened bread and bitter herbs. Do not eat any of it raw or boiled in water, but roasted over the fire, with its head, legs, and inner organs. You shall let none of it remain until the morning; anything that remains until the morning you shall burn. This is how you shall eat it: your loins girded, your sandals on your feet, and your staff in your hand; and you shall eat it hurriedly. It is the passover of the Lord. For I will pass through the land of Egypt that night, and I will strike down every firstborn in the land of Egypt, both human beings and animals; on all the gods of Egypt I will execute judgments: I am the Lord. The blood shall be a sign for you on the houses where you live: when I see the blood, I will pass over you, and no plague shall destroy you when I strike the land of Egypt.

EXODUS 12:1, 3–13

The Passover began as an exercise in plague prevention. Other plagues had failed to stir the hardened heart of Pharaoh, whose Egyptian empire was largely dependent on Hebrew slaves, especially for brick making (Exodus 1:8–14). Moses was called to set God's people free and, having little initial success, plagues were sent to pester the population. These plagues were rivers turned to blood (7:14–24), frogs or other reptiles (7:25—8:15), gnats (vv. 16–19), flies (vv. 20–32), disease on livestock (9:1–7), boils (vv. 8–12), hail and thunder (vv. 13–35), locusts (10:1–20) and darkness (vv. 21–29). Pharaoh did not listen so there was one final plague, involving the systematic extermination of all firstborn sons (11:4–8). It is this final curse against which the resident aliens must take precautions, and Moses and Aaron give the instructions.

The first Passover was a practical event. Since the Israelites were about to flee in haste, lambs or goats had to be killed quickly and their blood used as marker paint. Sheep and goats were rarely distinguished at the time; when Jesus later speaks of the separating of the sheep and goats (Matthew 25:32), he is emphasizing the power and extent of God's discernment. There was no time for any priestly involvement or, on this occasion, any liturgical dimension. The head of the household killed and roasted the lamb almost immediately. In doing so, the fat and blood were dealt with (both were forbidden: see Genesis 9:4; Exodus 29:13). The meat could not be boiled (which took too long and required preparation) or eaten raw (unhygienic and reminiscent of the practices of other religions). It was eaten with unleavened bread—dough baked without yeast, which took less time to prepare and cooked more quickly but would not have risen. The bitter herbs were not particularly significant at the first Passover but they lightened the heavy meal of meat and bread. Unusually, the people had to rush their meal, dressed for departure, which they knew would have to be swift and efficient.

It is important to distinguish between various forms of the Passover meal. Few instructions were given for the first Passover, which served to fill the Hebrew slaves before their flight from Egypt into the wilderness. There were many subsequent celebrations of Passover, commemorating this exodus, which turned the meal into a festival rich in ritual and meaning. By the time Jesus celebrated a Passoverstyle meal with his disciples at the last supper, the Passover feast (*Pesach*) was cemented in tradition. Also, we should not forget the ways in which Passover is celebrated today, both by Jews and Christians. Yet whichever context for Passover we consider, there is an inevitable, unbreakable association with a meal shared among family, friends and strangers. Passover survives still, of course, but has quietly influenced every Christian feast, so that today our Christmas and Easter and Thanksgiving dinners, our wedding breakfasts and birthday parties, all owe something to the day when God called Israel out of Egypt, requiring them to gird their loins and dine in anticipation of freedom.

Father God, who gave your people the Passover of salvation, keep us fed with your Spirit so that we may be always ready to drop everything and do your will. Amen

MOSES' MANNA

The Israelites said to them, 'If only we had died by the hand of the Lord in the land of Egypt, when we sat by the fleshpots and ate our fill of bread; for you have brought us out into this wilderness to kill this whole assembly with hunger.' Then the Lord said to Moses, 'I am going to rain bread from heaven for you...' ... and in the morning there was a layer of dew around the camp. When the layer of dew lifted, there... was a fine flaky substance, as fine as frost on the ground... Morning by morning they gathered it, as much as each needed; but when the sun grew hot, it melted... The house of Israel called it manna; it was like coriander seed, white, and the taste of it was like wafers made with honey... The Israelites ate manna for forty years, until they came to a habitable land; they ate manna, until they came to the border of the land of Canaan.

EXODUS 16:3–4, 13–14, 21, 31, 35

What on earth is manna? In a book about food and drink in life and faith, we can hardly overlook it, even though no one really knows what this archetypal food from God is or was. One theory, mentioned by Miriam Vamosh in her delightful book *Food at the Time of the Bible*, is that it was a liquid form of carbohydrate secreted by insects that fed on the tamarisk tree. In the desert it soon dried, creating a sweet flaky substance, which (scientists have deduced) contained three kinds of sugar as well as pectin, which would suffice to sustain a starving people.[10]

Whatever manna was, it was a life-saving gift from God and was seen as such, certainly at first. After a while, the Israelites got literally fed up with it and complained, 'If only we had meat to eat! We remember the fish we used to eat in Egypt for nothing, the cucumbers, the melons, the leeks, the onions, and the garlic; but now our strength is dried up, and there is nothing at all but this manna' (Numbers 11:4–6). Since they ate it for 40 years, it is perhaps not surprising that they hankered after a little variety in their diet.

Discontent is hardly unusual; indeed, our culture today thrives on it. Advertisers encourage us to become unhappy with some aspect of our lives (our car or diet or furniture) by suggesting that there is something better and that we need it. Having sold it to us, we soon are persuaded to tire of something else and so the media continue to create and sustain discontent. As L. Shannon Jung puts it, 'We seem to trade on lack of enjoyment. If more is always better, then we never get enough.'[11] Yet all that we have comes from God, directly or indirectly, and discontent is a form of ingratitude, a denial of the divine. Monotonous as the wilderness diet may have been, the story of manna reminds us of the commitment to the Israelites' survival that God made by supplying them with food.

It all seems a long way from how we get our food today. The Israelites were hunter-gatherers in the true sense, but all we hunt now are bargains and we gather only in trolleys. Do you know where your food comes from? Do you know how many miles it has travelled since it was cooked or killed? Do you know at what cost to others it has been produced? Has it, for example, been 'fairly' traded? In recent years many people have begun to take an interest in these questions and it seems that food retailers are beginning to listen.

Despite the apparently insurmountable problems associated with the structures of society that determine where our food comes from and how much we pay for it, it is possible to reduce the gap between food production and consumption. In the depths of that gap we lose sight of our integrity and become blind buyers of whatever is convenient or tasty. Often, in buying food, we do not know what is good for us or for others. Yet we can grow some of our own food. We can buy food from sources we learn to understand and value. We can contemplate the way food is packaged, and where and when it was packaged, and we can discover where our food waste goes. Does it end up in a compost heap or in a landfill site or thrown into the sea? More importantly, perhaps, we can learn to share and to say grace, giving thanks, not in lip-service but in understanding, for the gifts we have, all of which come to us as modern manna, bestowed by God on his ungrateful children.

God, you feed and sustain us in body and spirit. Teach us discernment that we may live as those who have received much and who have much to give. As mustard seeds yield great trees, may we in small ways make a difference where neglect, injustice or exploitation prevail. Amen

CANAAN'S MILK AND HONEY

For the Israelites travelled for forty years in the wilderness, until all the nation, the warriors who came out of Egypt, perished, not having listened to the voice of the Lord. To them the Lord swore that he would not let them see the land that he had sworn to their ancestors to give us, a land flowing with milk and honey... The Lord said to Joshua, 'Today I have rolled away from you the disgrace of Egypt.' And so that place is called Gilgal to this day. While the Israelites were camped in Gilgal they kept the passover in the evening on the fourteenth day of the month in the plains of Jericho. On the day after the passover, on that very day, they ate the produce of the land, unleavened cakes and parched grain. The manna ceased on the day they ate the produce of the land, and the Israelites no longer had manna; they ate the crops of the land of Canaan that year.
JOSHUA 5:6, 9–12

Yesterday we saw how God provided manna in the wilderness for the Israelites, but eventually the manna supply ceased. This was not a judgment of God or a punishment, but the marking of a new era for the post-wilderness travellers. They had arrived in Canaan, a new home, where they would settle. Consequently, they were able to cultivate crops and rear animals, producing cereals and milk, so that they lived and ate differently. Until the entry into Canaan, the Passover had been a memorial of the flight from Egypt: in the wilderness its celebration could only focus on that dimension. In Canaan, the Passover takes on a new significance, for there is the result to celebrate too—the arrival as well as the departure. The Passover also becomes something of a harvest festival, as the crops (barley and wheat) are used to make unleavened cakes and parched grain. Thus they do not need manna any more; there is more and better to eat from the new land.

Their diet changed both practically and symbolically. In the wilderness, there was not much to thank God for (or so they thought). Manna was an emergency ration, a direct gift from God to keep them alive. Yet those whom it initially sustained, who turned away from God and his generous act of deliverance through the Sea of Reeds, ultimately died en route. The new generation arrived, settled and ate different food produced in a different way. The Israelites took into their own bodies a different form of God's bounty—bounty for which they had to work but which yielded so much more in variety and potential. The new life gave much for which to be grateful and the Passover gained a new identity as a feast of gratitude that future generations continued to celebrate.

Canaan is the 'promised land' and in this passage we see the promise fulfilled. When it was yet a distant but divine promise, Canaan had gained a reputation as 'the land of milk and honey'. We still use that phrase today to refer to somewhere, perhaps imaginary, that holds great promise of bounty and sweetness and nourishment. Canaan flows with milk and honey and the symbolism is of abundance. Milk came from sheep, goats or cattle, and involved hard work, and it is easy to forget that the imagery associated with shepherding in the Bible concerns the one who safeguards the flock of sheep not just for wool or meat but for milk, too. The 'honey' was not from cultivated bees, but wild insects that flourished where there were many fruit trees. Thus the land flowing with milk and honey is a reference to a fertile place where cattle can graze and fruit trees abound, not only providing nectar for bees but yielding fruit that, if pressed or squeezed, produced a sweet juice that the Israelites likened to honey. Not all 'honey' in the Bible is honey as we know it: some is likely to be liquid from squashed dates.[12]

God's promise of resources relates to the natural environment in which the Israelites found themselves: as they moved and circumstances changed, the Lord's provision varied. Today we live in lands that, by comparison, are deluged with milk and honey. We are fortunate and we must attribute our good fortune not simply to hard work or science, for our ability to grow produce and understand the health value of food is itself a divine gift of bounty and understanding. Yet it is all too easy to waste food or destroy its goodness: modern production methods used in manufacturing both milk and honey (involving pasteurization or homogenization) often deprive them of most of their vitamins, amino acids and other health-giving properties. Like the ancient Israelites, we need to learn to be grateful for the ways in which God supplies our changing circumstances, and remember that there is a price to pay when we abuse or deny God's munificence towards us.

Lord, you bestow upon us good things to eat and drink in every time, place and season. Teach us to value and give thanks for your bounty, that we may flourish in your image and to your glory. Amen

JEWISH FOOD LAWS

Any animal that has divided hoofs and is cloven-footed and chews the cud—such you may eat... You shall not eat the following: the camel... rock badger... hare... pig... Of their flesh you shall not eat, and their carcasses you shall not touch; they are unclean for you... Everything in the waters that does not have fins and scales is detestable to you... You shall regard as detestable among the birds... the eagle, the vulture, the osprey, the buzzard, the kite... every raven... the ostrich, the nighthawk, the seagull, the hawk... the little owl, the cormorant, the great owl, the water-hen, the desert owl, the carrion vulture, the stork, the heron... the hoopoe, and the bat... Among the winged insects... you may eat: the locust... bald locust... cricket... grasshopper... But all other winged insects that have four feet are detestable to you... These are unclean for you... the weasel, the mouse, the great lizard... the gecko, the land crocodile, the lizard, the sand-lizard, and the chameleon...

If an animal of which you may eat dies, anyone who touches its carcass shall be unclean until the evening.... Whatever moves on its belly, and whatever moves on all fours, or whatever has many feet, all the creatures that swarm upon the earth, you shall not eat; for they are detestable... This is the law pertaining to land animal and bird and every living creature that moves through the waters and every creature that swarms upon the earth, to make a distinction between the unclean and the clean, and between the living creature that may be eaten and the living creature that may not be eaten.

LEVITICUS 11:3–8, 12–23, 29–30, 39–42, 46–47 (ABRIDGED)

Have you seen (or tried) scorpions in candy, or chocolate ants, or even bacon and cheese flavour crickets (a strange blend of kosher and non-kosher food)? They all seem repulsive to me, but John the Baptist ate locusts (Mark 1:6) and there is still a market for such delicacies. In Western culture they are novelties, involving a sense of bravado, whereas in some Middle Eastern cultures such foodstuffs are perfectly normal. Every person and every culture has ideas, if not laws, about what may acceptably be eaten, and this edited passage from Leviticus provides us with the archetypal food law to which orthodox Jews still adhere.

While Jesus declared this law null and void (Mark 7:19), and Peter had a vision in which he learned that 'what God has made clean, you must not call profane' (Acts 10:9–16), we are still squeamish about certain edible beasts. We tend not to want to eat animals we would not touch, although we may also have difficulty eating animals that we consider 'cuddly'. When a child first discovers the connection between the gambolling lamb and mint sauce, it can be a painful learning experience. Meanwhile, some cultures happily eat dogs, monkeys or live fish (in the belief that they swim around in the belly making room for more food).

In 1870, on the 99th day of the Siege of Paris, the two elephants at the zoo, Castor and Pollux, found themselves on the Christmas day menu.[13] In spite of some claims that elephant's trunk is delicious, I'm sure that most of us would baulk at elephant stew unless we were really hungry—which is precisely the point. Pushed to extremes, we may even contemplate cannibalism, as did those on the *Medusa*, a French ship that was wrecked on the West Coast of Africa in July 1816 and immortalized in Theodore Gericault's painting *The Raft of the Medusa* (1819), on show at the Louvre. The Jewish kosher laws were devised for a wilderness people (note the references to lizards and so forth), and the prohibitions had an inbuilt divine wisdom that ran: 'Do not eat these even if you are really hungry, because they are bad for you.' Prohibition creates both attraction and repellence; as pork is forbidden meat to Jews, we can imagine the revulsion of Jesus' hearers when he told them that the prodigal son worked with and ate the food meant for swine (Luke 15:15–16).

In a modern, hygienic world of fridge-freezers and tinned food, food laws seem outdated, and some liberal Jews agree. These laws were not simply for health reasons, however, but to remind the Israelites of the covenantal relationship between God and his chosen people. What they ate and what they refused to eat would remind them of this relationship every time they ate a meal—and this is still the case. There is also something to be said for a moral approach to what we consume. Food is essential to existence but, rather like matrimony, the relationship between ourselves and what we eat should not be 'enterprised, nor taken in hand, unadvisedly, lightly, or wantonly, but reverently, discreetly, advisedly, soberly, and in the fear of God; duly considering the causes for which food was ordained' (see the Book of Common Prayer Marriage Service).

Paul wrote, 'Food is meant for the stomach and the stomach for food' (1 Corinthians 6:13), but what and how we eat reveals our social and personal ethics. Many have principled preferences, while others are merely fussy. We know what we like and we live in a world where choice takes charge. Nevertheless, we are accountable for our choices, for the way they affect our environment, our neighbours and ourselves. Our bodies are members of Christ (1 Corinthians 6:15), and when we make our choices in a world without rules, we should remember that.

Father God, who blesses us with more than we need, guide and protect us in our food choices, that we may eat not only for ourselves but for the good of all creation. Amen

SOLOMON'S KITCHEN

Judah and Israel… ate and drank and were happy. Solomon was sovereign over all the kingdoms from the Euphrates to the land of the Philistines, even to the border of Egypt; they brought tribute and served Solomon all the days of his life. Solomon's provision for one day was thirty cors of choice flour, and sixty cors of meal, ten fat oxen, and twenty pasture-fed cattle, one hundred sheep, besides deer, gazelles, roebucks, and fatted fowl… Judah and Israel lived in safety, from Dan even to Beer-sheba, all of them under their vines and fig trees. Solomon also had forty thousand stalls of horses for his chariots, and twelve thousand horsemen. Those officials supplied provisions for King Solomon and for all who came to King Solomon's table, each one in his month; they let nothing be lacking. They also brought to the required place barley and straw for the horses and swift steeds.

I KINGS 4:20–23, 25–28 (ABRIDGED)

Living as we do in the prosperous West, we are very familiar with shopping lists, even one as ancient as Solomon's. The varied and copious foodstuffs available to him do not quite compare with the vast array of goods available in a supermarket today, and even Solomon in all his finery was susceptible to seasonal variations. Nowadays, the words 'seasonal food' do not indicate products that are 'in season', but are a marketing hype designating a section of the supermarket for Hallowe'en sweeties, Christmas cakes, Easter eggs, Mothering Sunday flowers, Father's Day real ale, Valentine's Day chocolates or New Year champagne.

Thanks largely to our supermarkets, feasting in our society has become associated with excess rather than with celebration. Seventy per cent of the groceries bought in the UK come from the biggest four supermarket retailers, giving them a massive influence not only over what we eat and how much we pay for it (an issue in itself), but also over our attitude towards religious and secular festivals. Most of our festive seasons have been converted into opportunities to consume extra chocolate and alcohol and, in the case of Hallowe'en, supermarkets and other retailers have done a disgraceful job of turning a celebration of what is good into a glorification of that which is evil.

Notwithstanding the flaws of supermarket culture, we have to acknowledge their convenience and ability to supply a range of goods and foodstuffs that would have confounded even King Solomon. Each day, his large entourage of courtiers, servants, soldiers and huntsmen got through thousands of litres of flour. There was plenty of meat on the tables and acres of space on which the annual requirement of 3650 oxen, 36,500 sheep and 7200 cattle might roam. Even if some of these figures are exaggerated, we get a sense of an expensive, large-scale operation that could only really be sustained in peace-time.

As with our supermarkets, high and varied demand and supply can be met only where trade and resources are secure. Solomon, like us, lived in relative security and peace. Supermarkets abound today in the EU and USA, which have enjoyed peace and economic growth since 1945. Prosperity soon evolves into complacency and then gluttony, however, which produces a vast amount of waste. We may well wonder, inferring from our own context, whether Solomon's kitchens generated a lot of waste. We may also remind ourselves that, in spite of what moralizing politicians may say, most wars are fought over resources, and the most important resources are water, land and food. It has been argued that the genocide in Rwanda in 1996, for example, was largely a fight for water. In 1992 Rwanda had the fastest-growing population in the world, with an average of eight children for each woman. Food production could not keep up and water resources were stretched. The resulting war between the Hutu and Tutsi tribes, which cost two million lives, may have had at its root a struggle for access to resources.[14]

Water is not only the juice of life: we need it for our own uses but it is also necessary for crops and animals. Solomon must have had access to large reserves of it. While oil is often cited as a cause of war, especially in the Middle East, it is a means to an end, enabling us to eat, travel and fight wars. Recent increases in fuel costs remind us of our dependence on oil, reflected directly in increases in the global cost of food, which is also affected by the recent enthusiasm for alternative fuels created from crops. Bio-fuel production itself also causes food shortages worldwide as the amount of land used to feed increasing populations is reduced. Bio-fuels are disastrous because they inhibit food supply in the face of increased demand. When fuel is short for whatever reason, people complain that they can't go shopping, not only because they cannot drive to the supermarket but because the shelves are empty. Fuel crises cause lack of food in our interconnected wealthy world, and food shortages are not something that any civilized government can countenance. Solomon ensured that his people were well fed, and thus presided over one of the greatest periods of prosperity in their history.

Solomon seems wealthy and generous, spending all this money on his people. Yet his money came from them and they effectively permitted him to be so generous. They liked living well, so the relationship between leader and people flourished. Leaders who keep the table full are invariably popular, whether elected or not. Economic prosperity prevents revolutions and wins votes. Poverty and starvation breed unrest, bloodshed and insecurity. As Christians we should pray for, fund and promote charities and organizations that assist and enable the building and sustenance of stable societies, who will need to seek emergency aid less frequently.

Munificent God, grant that all your people may live in prosperity and peace, ever mindful of your bountiful goodness towards us revealed in creation and incarnation. Amen

Friday

ELISHA'S POISONED STEW

When Elisha returned to Gilgal, there was a famine in the land. As the company of prophets was sitting before him, he said to his servant, 'Put the large pot on, and make some stew for the company of prophets.' One of them went out into the field to gather herbs; he found a wild vine and gathered from it a lapful of wild gourds, and came and cut them up into the pot of stew, not knowing what they were. They served some for the men to eat. But while they were eating the stew, they cried out, 'O man of God, there is death in the pot!' They could not eat it. He said, 'Then bring some flour.' He threw it into the pot, and said, 'Serve the people and let them eat.' And there was nothing harmful in the pot.

2 KINGS 4:38–41

I am not much of a gardener, and the few things I am interested in growing tend to be things I can eat. Not long ago, we grew some courgettes and gourds in our garden, and eventually they bore fruit and we began to enjoy fresh produce. The gourd plant produced only one vegetable, which, when it reached the size of a large orange, I picked, peeled, seeded, chopped and boiled. My wife and daughter showed little interest in dining off this amazing plant so I ate most of it. I was ill for three days. Apparently our neighbours had given it to my wife to plant as an 'ornamental' gourd!

I cannot be sure it was the gourd that made me ill, any more than we can say with certainty what kind of gourd it was that Elisha's servant fetched for the stew. Most scholars have suggested it was *citrullus colocynthis*, a relative of the watermelon, sometimes called 'bitter apple', and known in biblical times as 'wild gourd' or 'gall'. It was possibly from the same fruit that the juice that Jesus was offered on the cross was taken ('they offered him wine to drink, mixed with gall; but when he tasted it, he would not drink it': Matthew 27:34), although some say that it might have been myrrh mixed with the wine.

The fruit of *citrullus colocynthis* is basically poisonous. It can be used cautiously as a medicine for stomach pains or as a laxative, and the seeds are edible if ground to make bread. They also produce a rich oil, which can also be used to make candles. Small amounts of the fruit can be used as a moth deterrent. If consumed in large amounts, however, the fruit can cause bloody discharges and can be deadly. Opium is often suggested as an antidote.

It is therefore not surprising that Elisha's guests were alarmed, being offered mothball stew by an unwitting cook. Yet Elisha was able to act quickly and apparently miraculously to save them and the dish. A similar thing happened in the wilderness immediately after the Israelites had fled from the Egyptians. The water in the wilderness of Shur was bitter but God showed Moses a piece of wood to throw into the water to make it safe to drink (see Exodus 15:22–25). As in our story of Elisha, whatever the properties of the wood may have been, there was a deeper meaning, which Moses made explicit: 'If you will listen carefully to the voice of the Lord your God, and do what is right in his sight, and give heed to his commandments and keep all his statutes, I will not bring upon you any of the diseases that I brought upon the Egyptians; for I am the Lord who heals you' (v. 26).

On one level, the moral of Elisha's tale is the same for me with my ornamental gourd as it was for Elisha's servants who went foraging: do not cook and eat stuff when you do not know what it is! Not all nature is for our good, and some mushrooms and fruits are deadly. More importantly, this incident demonstrates Elisha's prowess as a man of God. In what seemed like danger, brought on by foolishness, he knew what to do and acted fast. His solution was simple and effective.

Yet there is a third, symbolic way in which to read this story, for in

Elisha's time there was famine in the land. (This story is immediately followed by an account of the prophet feeding 100 men with only 20 loaves of barley, prefiguring Jesus' feeding miracles.) The famine may have been physical but it also represents a spiritual famine, as the people were not being fed with proper teaching from the very prophets whom Elisha was feeding. The wild gourds represent false teachings which, although innocently thrown into the pot, bring 'death' and 'poison' to the healthy word of God. Elisha's solution is to throw in good flour and, as Christians, we might want to go so far as to associate this with Jesus, the true food who purges the poison of secular society and renders cynicism impotent, bringing new life where there has previously only been death and sin.

Lord Christ, purge away the impurities and poisons of our lives, and fill us with the good food of the gospel. Amen

THE PSALMIST'S TABLE

The Lord is my shepherd, I shall not want. He makes me lie down in green pastures; he leads me beside still waters; he restores my soul. He leads me in right paths for his name's sake. Even though I walk through the darkest valley, I fear no evil; for you are with me; your rod and your staff—they comfort me. You prepare a table before me in the presence of my enemies; you anoint my head with oil; my cup overflows. Surely goodness and mercy shall follow me all the days of my life, and I shall dwell in the house of the Lord my whole life long.

PSALM 23

For some people Lent is all about food, but for others life is all about food. Food can be the delight or the bane of someone's life. While 1.1 billion people in the world do not have enough to eat, others in the more affluent West suffer from conditions that are as much psychological as physical—anorexia and obesity, both of which, like hunger, cause the sufferer to spend most of the waking day dealing with the difficulties that the business of eating presents.

Anorexia is not as common as obesity but it can be equally debilitating and deadly. Anorexia sufferers, the majority of whom are women, are not simply trying to make themselves thin; there can be deeper issues about insecurity, lack of self-esteem, and the need for love and value lurking underneath self-starvation. As L. Shannon Jung puts it, 'each of the victims of disorder (has) an intense longing for connection with other people. In literally no case did any victims of eating disorders feel a strong sense of community with others.'[15] Anorexia is truly a tragic illness and the road to recovery is long, requiring patience, love and mental and spiritual care as well as a dietary regime. Anorexics often display behaviour like that of addicts: secretly not eating, making themselves sick (sometimes referred to as bulimia, which is also a separate condition), overexercising, and obsessive calorie-counting. As in the case of those who are addicted to alcohol or an illegal substance, other members of the family often find themselves drawn into a life of cajoling, secrecy, deceit, despair, guilt and retribution. Tough as this can be, anorexia can be treated, but it takes a great deal of determination, love, encouragement and not a little food.

Obesity appears on the other side of the coin and is far more common. Thirty-one per cent of Americans are obese, and 22 per cent of Britons. Strictly speaking, a person is obese if their body weight is more than 20 per cent what it should be, given height, gender, age and build. Obesity is dangerous because it increases the likelihood of strokes, diabetes, heart attacks, gout, cancer, gallstones and osteoarthritis. It is remarkable how many people in the Western world are obese (as opposed to merely overweight), given these known risks. This indicates that being obese is not best thought of as a matter of choice, for the way our society is structured promotes obesity in communities and individuals.

Our society is full of food and our economies are structured to provide the well-fed with more and the hungry with less. As a nation, we should work towards altering those economic structures that create and sustain excessive consumption, and we should treat this as a spiritual and moral imperative. The Bible has always advocated care for the poor, needy and hungry and, while the circumstances of today may be complex and different, the basic principles of care and compassion are just as important.

The psalmist, we can safely presume, knew nothing about eating disorders or modern politics but he did know about hunger, greed and injustice. His words about a banquet spread near the valley of death are poignant and pertinent for our time. Those who suffer severely from eating disorders do walk in the valley of death when the thought of a banquet causes a near-phobic anticipation of weight gain and humiliation. Their souls may truly need to be restored by God's touch. We too need to be led into right paths when our diet is governed by lack of self-control, greed or ingratitude, or when it leads to social injustice, exclusion and death. Psalm 23 presents us with a grateful vision of peace, plenty and deliverance. May it inspire us in the search for healing and wholeness for nations and individuals who are damaged by desire or by disregard for the good things the Lord spreads before us.

God of justice, banish from your people all greed and ungraciousness, and heal the diseases of plenty, that individuals and communities may live and dine together in your love that casts out fear, until we behold the heavenly table that you spread in the face of every people. Amen

WEEK THREE

ISAIAH'S VINEYARD

My beloved had a vineyard on a very fertile hill. He dug it and cleared it of stones, and planted it with choice vines; he built a watch-tower in the midst of it, and hewed out a wine vat in it; he expected it to yield grapes, but it yielded wild grapes... I will tell you what I will do to my vineyard. I will remove its hedge, and it shall be devoured; I will break down its wall, and it shall be trampled down. I will make it a waste; it shall not be pruned or hoed, and it shall be overgrown with briers and thorns; I will also command the clouds that they rain no rain upon it. For the vineyard of the Lord of hosts is the house of Israel, and the people of Judah are his pleasant planting; he expected justice, but saw bloodshed; righteousness, but heard a cry!

ISAIAH 5:1–2, 5–7

Isaiah's diatribe against the people of Judah, condemning them for their lack of justice and prophesying their doom at the hands of invading armies, contains this metaphorical description of the nation as the vineyard of the Lord. This analogy pervades the Bible: as the Canadian writer Tom Harpur says, 'The Bible is literally drenched in wine.'[16] Jesus draws on it in his parables of the wicked tenants (Matthew 21:33–41) and the workers in the vineyard (20:1–16). While Noah is described as the first to plant a vineyard (Genesis 9:20; also see 'Noah gets drunk', p. 30), the inability of a wandering or exiled people to plant a vineyard was seen as a sort of curse (Jeremiah 35:1–10).

A key theme in Isaiah's vine imagery is that of judgment. While the abundance of wine symbolized hope and blessing, the lack of it or the destruction of vines signalled God's wrath. Where vines prosper, there is goodness and joy ('Your wife will be like a fruitful vine within your house': Psalm 128:3), and we can remember Joseph correctly interpreting Pharaoh's cupbearer's dream about flourishing vines to signify restoration and redemption (Genesis 40).

Isaiah's description gives an insight into ancient Middle Eastern viniculture. The grapes were *vitis vinifera sylvestris,* originally from Turkey, Armenia and Iran. The 'Syrah' or 'Shiraz' grape is a descendant of those grapes, and Shiraz is still the name of an Iranian city. Back in ancient Israel, the harvest was welcomed with feasting and the grapes were put into open-air presses in the hills. Before presses were developed, pressing took place underfoot, an approach still valued today as it avoids breaking the pips, releasing tannin, oil and seeds. Yeast conveniently occurs naturally in wineskins, which begin the process of fermentation in the juice as soon as the grapes are pressed. Most grapes were red—white grapes are produced by a recessive gene—thus inviting an obvious association with blood ('I trampled down peoples in my anger, I crushed them in my wrath, and I poured out their lifeblood on the earth': Isaiah 63:6). Wine could be drunk young or old, though new wine should not be put into old wineskins (Luke 5:37), and some wine travelled well: Hosea drank wine from Lebanon (Hosea 14:7), a region that still produces excellent and reasonably priced wine today.

As we saw when we looked at Noah's wine making, the benefits of wine were recognized for both healing and drinking, but it could also be harmful. Perhaps the best advice comes from the writer of Ecclesiasticus (Sirach), who tells us, 'Wine is very life to human beings if taken in moderation. What is life to one who is without wine? It has been created to make people happy. Wine drunk at the proper time and in moderation is rejoicing of heart and gladness of soul' (Sirach 31:27).

We are still very much surrounded by wine today. In spite of times of prohibition and high taxation, wine drinking is a popular and pleasant pastime, and vintage wine is a sound investment, with some wines commanding extremely high prices. French culture and economics are wine-orientated, with a highly structured categorization of the Bordeaux Châteaux (Lafite-Rothschild, Margaux, Latour, Haut-Brion, Yquem and Mouton-Rothschild being the most senior). Premier Cru through to Cinquieme Cru (the Grands Cru) are succeeded in the Médoc region by Cru Bourgeois, with St Emilion wines having their own classifications as Premier Grand Cru Classé (Class A or B) and Grand Cru Classé. Wine is also distinguished by grape type, there being about 40 kinds of red wine grape and 50 white that are commonly used worldwide. From sweet ice-wine and sauternes through to dry clarets, and with fortified ports and sherries, there is plenty of choice.

Many of these wines owe their heritage to *vitis vinifera sylvestris*, which, like God's word, has spread, adapted, been cultivated, propagated and enjoyed worldwide, producing much fruit, with which body and soul are blessed. As wine is a constant in the Bible, so too are the key themes of God's bounty leading to celebration and rejoicing, allied with judgment, through which God calls us to repent and return to him.

God our Father, as you tend and nurture your heavenly vineyard, in your mercy prune away our sin and restore us to righteousness, that we may lead lives of justice and moderation, to your glory. Amen

ISAIAH'S FEAST

Ho, everyone who thirsts, come to the waters; and you that have no money, come, buy and eat! Come, buy wine and milk without money and without price. Why do you spend your money for that which is not bread, and your labour for that which does not satisfy? Listen carefully to me, and eat what is good, and delight yourselves in rich food. Incline your ear, and come to me; listen, so that you may live. I will make with you an everlasting covenant, my steadfast, sure love for David... Seek the Lord while he may be found, call upon him while he is near... For my thoughts are not your thoughts, nor are your ways my ways, says the Lord.

ISAIAH 55:1–3, 6, 8

The German statistician Ernst Engel (1821–96) proposed what is now known as Engel's Law, which states that the lower a family's income, the greater is the proportion that is spent on food. A family must eat and, no matter how wealthy you are, food costs the same, so it is extremely likely that poorer families will spend proportionately more on food than richer families. In 1997 the United States Agricultural Department (USDA) published research indicating that the populations of rich countries spend 16 per cent of their income on food, while the people of poor nations spend 55 per cent.[17] If we consider the UK, a rich nation, we would therefore expect a sixth of our income to be spent on food, but we find that by 2007 individuals were spending, on average, a total of £443 a week, with £62 being spent on travel and £58 on recreation, culture and leisure. Purchases of food came third, averaging £45 a week— about ten per cent of income, a percentage of income spent on food even smaller than the previous 16 per cent. (The figures are slightly different for families with two children, where the total weekly spend averages £642 per week.)[18] According to Engel's Law, then, the UK has become significantly richer in the space of ten years.

While the fact that our food, on which our bodies and mental health depend, is not our primary expenditure is interesting in itself, the notion that we spend more on getting around and enjoying ourselves says something about the priorities of life today. Furthermore, if we total the amounts spent on these three aspects of life, there is a considerable environmental impact made by each of us, as food production, travel and leisure activities all consume energy.

Isaiah has something to say about our priorities, for today we certainly spend our money on 'that which is not bread', and the way in which we do so says something about our spiritual lives. A decision about what to buy can become all-consuming: if we need to change our car, television or washing machine, there is so much choice. There are shops to visit, brochures to read, people to consult, websites to browse. Shopping can be quite good fun, and we often spend time as well as money doing it because it is important not to waste money. But shopping can also become addictive. Sometimes we don't know when to stop, when to make the purchase and get on with life. Yet, as James asks us, where does all this fit into the divine plan and the scale of eternity?

Come now, you who say, 'Today or tomorrow we will go to such and such a town and spend a year there, doing business and making money.' Yet you do not even know what tomorrow will bring. What is your life? For you are a mist that appears for a little while and then vanishes. (James 4:13–14)

We should be investing our wealth in that which satisfies, and, while Isaiah uses the metaphor of food, he is actually making a spiritual recommendation. The feast to which God is inviting the Israelites through Isaiah is a spiritual feast, where the flowing wine and milk represent God's outpouring of spiritual goodness and pleasure. We do need to shop for food, drink and other commodities, but we also need to 'seek the Lord', 'incline our ears to the word of God', and live in the light of his covenantal love.

Just as we need the spiritual sustenance that comes from God, we need the physical sustenance of food. Yet Isaiah's food imagery turns a basic need into a lavish extravagance as we are invited to consume the richest of food. This may surprise us, who are aware of a long ascetic tradition in Christianity, of monastic meagreness and the frugality that accompanied many ecclesiastical and spiritual movements throughout history. Isaiah's words challenge and overturn that idea with a banquet of quality and quantity. It is not simply spiritual food on offer, but superlative spiritual food, the best wine and freshest milk, not only for satisfying hunger but also to delight the palate. In an earlier passage from Isaiah, the same promise is made: 'On this mountain the Lord of hosts will make for all peoples a feast of rich food, a feast of well-matured wines, of rich food filled with marrow, of well-matured wines strained clear' (25:6). Bread and water will satisfy hunger but God offers so much more than mere satisfaction.

Bountiful God, help us to assess our spiritual and material priorities, that we may seek first the wine of your kingdom and the milk of your loving kindness. Amen

ISAIAH'S FAST

Shout out, do not hold back! Lift up your voice like a trumpet! Announce to my people their rebellion, to the house of Jacob their sins. Yet day after day they seek me and delight to know my ways, as if they were a nation that practised righteousness and did not forsake the ordinance of their God; they ask of me righteous judgments, they delight to draw near to God. 'Why do we fast, but you do not see? Why humble ourselves, but you do not notice?' Look, you serve your own interest on your fast-day, and oppress all your workers. Look, you fast only to quarrel and to fight and to strike with a wicked fist. Such fasting as you do today will not make your voice heard on high. Is such the fast that I choose, a day to humble oneself? Is it to bow down the head like a bulrush, and to lie in sackcloth and ashes? Will you call this a fast, a day acceptable to the Lord? Is not this the fast that I choose: to loose the bonds of injustice, to undo the thongs of the yoke, to let the oppressed go free, and to break every yoke? Is it not to share your bread with the hungry, and bring the homeless poor into your house; when you see the naked, to cover them, and not to hide yourself from your own kin? Then your light shall break forth like the dawn, and your healing shall spring up quickly; your vindicator shall go before you, the glory of the Lord shall be your rearguard.

ISAIAH 58:1–8

Just as our approach to feasting has origins in Jewish practice, so do our attitudes towards fasting. And just as feasting is not simply about eating lots and having fun, fasts are not entirely about refraining from food but have other meanings and purposes. The removal of food-stuffs from the diet is a form of fast. It is a technique that Hippocrates employed two and a half millennia ago, which is still used for both religious and health reasons today. What we eat can aggravate or alleviate medical conditions. For example, arthritis sufferers are sometimes advised to 'fast' from particular 'food families', confining themselves to pears and sweet potatoes, and from that baseline to introduce foods in order to discover and eliminate those that 'upset the system'. Bread, wheat and yeast can cause problems, and many church leaders are now familiar with the coeliac condition that prevents people from even consuming a Communion wafer because of the allergic reaction to gluten that it can cause. It is possible to get gluten-free wafers to avoid the spiritual and physical dilemmas brought on by an inability to consume the bread of Holy Communion.

Fasting has biblical origins too: at Bethel the Israelites wept before the Lord and fasted for a day (Judges 20:26) and other biblical fasts lasted for periods of three to 40 days. While fasting is most often associated with spiritual cleansing, devotion or self-discipline, we can easily forget how healthy it can be, whether it be a complete fast (abstaining from all food) for a brief period or a more extended partial fast. As Dr Rex Russell puts it, 'Fasting helps unclog the system, and also eliminates poison from it... Modern research, ancient healers and more importantly the word of the body's Designer—God—indicate that one benefit of fasting is healing.'[19] Fasting also focuses the mind and may benefit mental health. Spiritually speaking, fasting helps us to focus on God, to pray, to remove from our cluttered imaginations the cares of the world.

On the other hand, fasting induces hunger (or even hypoglycemic reactions in some, who may have inadvertently become dependent on sugars), and this can cause headaches and irritability, such that the desire to break the fast can become overbearing. To overcome this difficulty requires not only determination but also bodily training, so that we learn gradually to reduce our dependency on addictive substances like sugar, fat or caffeine. We may have to do this before attempting a serious fast. Fasting can help to conquer such addictions but it is physically and mentally difficult to do so, which is probably why fasting is an alien concept to so many people today.

However, more people are rediscovering the spiritual and physical benefits of fasting, whether for health reasons, to promote spiritual growth or as a gesture of solidarity with the weak and poor. Hunger lunches and other communal meals, where little or nothing is eaten by some or all present, highlight food justice issues, sometimes raising money as well as awareness of others' needs. As Isaiah pointed out, fasting without justice is hypocritical, since fasting was not only for healing but also in order to focus on the need to feed others and to seek to break the bonds of oppression. Indeed, the one follows the other.

Lord, help us to remove from our bodies and souls anything that turns us away from you or makes us dependent on our own desires. When fasting, help us to focus on you, that we may be healed in heart and mind, purified for your Spirit's presence within us. Amen

EZEKIEL'S RECIPE

Take wheat and barley, beans and lentils, millet and spelt; put them into one vessel, and make bread for yourself. During the number of days that you lie on your side, three hundred and ninety days, you shall eat it. The food that you eat shall be twenty shekels a day by weight; at fixed times you shall eat it. And you shall drink water by measure, one-sixth of a hin; at fixed times you shall drink. You shall eat it as a barley-cake, baking it in their sight on human dung. The Lord said, 'Thus shall the people of Israel eat their bread, unclean, among the nations to which I will drive them.' Then I said, 'Ah Lord God! I have never defiled myself; from my youth up until now I have never eaten what died of itself or was torn by animals, nor has carrion flesh come into my mouth.' Then he said to me, 'See, I will let you have cow's dung instead of human dung, on which you may prepare your bread.'

EZEKIEL 4:9–15

Ezekiel's ministry lasted about 22 years (592–573BC), a remarkable achievement for an exile. He settled with others at Tel Aviv on the banks of the river Chebar (not the same place as the modern Israeli city, the name of which was inspired by Ezekiel 3:15). He had a house in Babylon (8:1) and was married, but his wife died suddenly (24:18). His wife's death became meaningful in terms of the wider fate of Israel, as did other events of his life, for Ezekiel was a prophet whose actions were almost as important as his words. Here he bakes bread according to a command of the Lord, in order to remind his fellow exiles of the recipe for disaster produced by their idolatry and disloyalty. He hopes also to inspire them (and us) with the clarity and hope contained in his vision of a restored, rejuvenated and renewed relationship with God.

The making of bread in Ezekiel's time was a painstaking task. It was generally women's work, so it is significant that Ezekiel, a male prophet, bakes it, undertaking a task that he would not normally do, even though he evidently knows how. His bread contains ingredients that were then available only in Babylon—such as spelt, a type of wheat—but his recipe can be reproduced today.

Take 200g of durum wheat flour, 100g each of barley flour and ground lentil flour and 50g each of millet flour and ground broad bean flour, mix them and add a teaspoonful of salt. (These flours can be purchased in health food shops or ground manually.) Then add a quarter of a cup of olive oil, and water to dampen the mixture. If this is your first batch of dough, add half a cupful of freshly squeezed apple or grape juice. It must be fresh and home-pressed because these fruits have natural yeast in their skins, which 'contaminates' the juice when pressed, and this must go into the mixture to create leaven. After mixing everything together, knead it into dough and keep it warm for a couple of hours. It should rise a little. If you wish to make more bread later, remove some of the dough and keep it to add into the next batch: this is how it was done in biblical times, when one lump of dough would leaven the next preparation. Knead the remaining dough again and make small, flat, oval loaves. Bake the bread on hot coals or embers, or in a hot oven, until golden brown.

This is the easy way, of course, as we begin with ready-ground flour. In biblical times, breadmaking began with wheat or barley grain being ground into flour by hand. The grinding stone was a critical household tool, so much so that it was forbidden to offer it as security for a loan: 'No one shall take a mill or an upper millstone in pledge, for that would be taking a life in pledge' (Deuteronomy 24:6). The flour was mixed with water and kneaded together with leaven as above. Leaven took three weeks to mature from a piece of old dough in which yeast had naturally formed. The process from grinding to baking took a long time, and would require an early start for the woman of the house: 'She rises while it is still night and provides food for her household' (Proverbs 31:15). To feed half a dozen people could take up to three hours' preparation.

Baking was done in a clay or mud and straw oven, and was quite quick. The oven was usually outside in the courtyard, which meant that baking was a public business. Hence the injunction to Ezekiel to use human dung: everyone would have noticed his unsavoury approach. Indeed, it was so unpleasant that Ezekiel protested and, in virtue of his own righteousness, was permitted to use the more conventional cow dung as fuel for the fire.

Ezekiel's public exercise in baking was one of many prophetic acts. Elsewhere, he eats a scroll (3:3), sketches Jerusalem on a brick (4:1), shaves his head (5:1), lies on his left side for 390 days and his right side for 40 (4:4–8), digs through a wall twice (8:8; 12:7) and writes on two sticks (37:15–17). These actions serve to indicate to his people that they have offended God, and that their exile, during which they will have to eat bread cooked in this unclean manner (using 'dirty' fuel), is the righteous judgment of God upon their sinfulness. Nowadays we shy away from suggesting that God judges individuals and communities in this kind of way, but we are sometimes called to endure hardship, humiliation or unpleasant circumstances. We may have the opportunity to avoid this kind of thing if we turn away from what is right, but if we truly want to help those in need—even within our own families, perhaps—it may become our daily bread to have to roll our sleeves up, work hard at unpleasant tasks and get dirty in the service of others and God.

God of mercy and justice, show pity towards those who have no bread and give us grace to amend our ways and listen to your voice wherever it may be heard. Amen

DANIEL'S FAST

Daniel resolved that he would not defile himself with the royal rations of food and wine; so he asked the palace master to allow him not to defile himself. Now God allowed Daniel to receive favour and compassion from the palace master. The palace master said to Daniel, 'I am afraid of my lord the king; he has appointed your food and your drink. If he should see you in poorer condition than the other young men of your own age, you would endanger my head with the king.' Then Daniel asked the guard whom the palace master had appointed over Daniel, Hananiah, Mishael, and Azariah: 'Please test your servants for ten days. Let us be given vegetables to eat and water to drink. You can then compare our appearance with the appearance of the young men who eat the royal rations, and deal with your servants according to what you observe.' So he agreed to this proposal and tested them for ten days. At the end of ten days it was observed that they appeared better and fatter than all the young men who had been eating the royal rations. So the guard continued to withdraw their royal rations and the wine they were to drink, and gave them vegetables.

DANIEL 1:8–16

The Vegetarian Society of the United Kingdom claims to be the oldest vegetarian society in the world, representing four million British vegetarians (see www.vegsoc.org). In May 1999 they offered the nation 99 reasons for becoming vegetarian. Vegetarians are healthier, using hospitals 22 per cent less than others, suffering less from cancer, heart disease, high blood pressure, osteoporosis, gallstones, obesity, Type II diabetes, food poisoning and various forms of dementia. Vegetarians also have to spend less money on food and have a lower impact on the environment. It is not true, apparently, that vegetarians are weak or unfit.

While the story about Daniel and his companions refusing the royal food seems to underline these two common misconceptions about vegetarianism, the text is not a polemical tale about refusing to eat meat. It may seem that the story serves to support the view that abstaining from meat is not linked to physical weakness, and that if we eat only vegetables we will be healthier. This passage, with which the book of Daniel begins, is in fact more about idolatry and kingship than about vegetarianism or even Jewish food laws. Jewish diets included meat and there were no prohibitions against meat *per se*, although pork was forbidden (Deuteronomy 14:8). The Babylonians did eat pork so it is possible that Daniel rejected the meat because he did not know what it was. More significantly, he would not have known whether it had been sacrificed to idols, and therefore did not want to risk being tainted by unholy food. The apostle Paul, writing to the Corinthians, reveals that the eating of food offered to false gods was still an issue in the first century AD. Quoting an adage, he says, 'Food will not bring us close to God', but adds, 'If food is a cause of their falling, I will never eat meat, so that I may not cause one of them to fall' (1 Corinthians 8:8, 13). He could equally well be expressing the thoughts of Daniel, who needs to preserve his integrity not only for himself but for Hananiah, Mishael and Azariah (also known as Shradrach, Meshach and Abednego: see Daniel 1:7).

More important still is the issue of whom Daniel and his friends serve. Fit and clever members of the Israelite nobility, the men were taken from a besieged Jerusalem in 605BC to the heart of the Babylonian empire, ruled by King Nebuchadnezzar. Fêted and well fed, the plan was to integrate and employ them in the king's court. Not only were they prize captives but their submission would underline the absolute victory of an apparently civilized and benevolent invader. Thus, for both political and religious reasons, Daniel and his friends do not comply with every regulation imposed on them. In a daring move, they are not so crass as to go on hunger strike but they use their diet as a means to resist complete assimilation into Babylonian culture. In doing so, they succeed both in impressing their masters and in keeping faith with God, subtly proving that they do not need the favours of Nebuchadnezzar but have a heavenly king who protects and prospers them. This is to become a theme for the book of Daniel. The fact that they gain weight is therefore not a vegetarian manifesto but a demonstration of the power of God to maintain them even in the face of the contemporaneous opinion that vegetarians do not thrive.

For us today, as for Daniel, it is most important to have integrity in our worship and lifestyle, and this may mean that we become vegetarians for one of 99 reasons. Vegetarians have a particular integrity that should be respected by those who know that such a lifestyle demands sacrifices they themselves are not willing or able to make.

God of all creation, give us integrity and wisdom in the way we order our lives, in what we eat and drink, and in what we say and pray. Help us when we are weak, that in all things we may serve only you. Amen

BELSHAZZAR'S FEAST

King Belshazzar made a great festival... Under the influence of the wine, Belshazzar commanded that they bring in the vessels of gold and silver that his father Nebuchadnezzar had taken out of the temple in Jerusalem, so that... [they] might drink from them... They drank the wine and praised the gods of gold and silver, bronze, iron, wood, and stone. Immediately the fingers of a human hand appeared and began writing... Then all the king's wise men came in, but they could not read the writing or tell the king the interpretation. Then King Belshazzar became greatly terrified...

Then Daniel was brought in before the king... [He said] 'O king, the Most High God gave your father Nebuchadnezzar kingship, greatness, glory, and majesty... But when his heart was lifted up and his spirit was hardened so that he acted proudly, he was deposed from his kingly throne, and his glory was stripped from him... And you, Belshazzar his son, have not humbled your heart, even though you knew all this! ... So from [God's] presence the hand was sent and this writing was inscribed... MENE, MENE, TEKEL, and PARSIN. This is the interpretation of the matter: MENE, God has numbered the days of your kingdom and brought it to an end; TEKEL, you have been weighed on the scales and found wanting; PERES, your kingdom is divided and given to the Medes and Persians.' ...

That very night Belshazzar, the Chaldean king, was killed.

DANIEL 5:1–5, 8–9, 13, 18–30 (ABRIDGED)

Hanging in my kitchen (where else?) is a copy of Rembrandt's painting *Belshazzar's Feast*, painted in 1635, which captures the moment when the mysterious hand writes on the wall. It must have been frightening, and Rembrandt's picture of the king portrays a man wide-eyed with fear and disbelief. Onlookers pause from their boozing and flinch in horror.

Belshazzar deserves all that he gets, however. The previous king, Nebuchadnezzar (probably not Belshazzar's actual father), brought Daniel and others to Babylon, expecting them to convert to his religion. He stole the liturgical vessels used in the Jerusalem temple and brought them to Babylon after Jerusalem was ransacked in 586BC (see 2 Kings 24). Belshazzar decides to bring them out for his party, thereby desecrating them.

A Christian parallel might be the use of Communion chalices for a pub crawl. Such acts of sacrilege are rare but profoundly upsetting. For this reason they hold a wicked attraction for those wanting to cause hurt or affront. Yet we must not forget that Belshazzar got drunk, and in that state people often do things they regret: what seems like harmless fun or a mild joke can, in the cold light of dawn, be mortifying to those who have lost control the previous night. Belshazzar only commands that the temple vessels be used after he has got drunk, but this is a crime so great that he will be punished. Being intoxicated is no excuse, any more than it is today.

There are three things we may learn from this Old Testament debauchery—first, that God punishes those who desecrate holiness. Belshazzar's fate is a severe one: death is the consequence of drunken desecration, but the story underlines the severity of what he did.

Second, we may detect a moral about what can happen under the severe influence not just of alcohol but of any mind-changing substance. Belshazzar abandons decency and dignity, losing control of himself and others. He is not fit to be king: his judgment and punishment are swift and conclusive.

Third, we are reminded of God's love and care for his people even in the face of ignominious humiliation. No matter how bad it is, no matter how weak God's people seem to have become, God is in and above and over all. God remains with us even in the face of what seems like absolute defeat or humiliation. This story of a Godinsulter reminded the Jewish exiles, and us today, of the powers to which we are allied.

As we recall this disastrous, destructive feast hosted by a Babylonian despot, let us also heed the warnings that lie behind it. It is by no means wrong to have a feast: each year has a few in store for us, Easter and Christmas among them. But feasting should not be so indulgent as to forget its origins or purpose, and it should never take us so far into gluttony or drunkenness that we denigrate or desecrate the truths on which we are called to build our lives. All good things come from God, and it is with goodness of heart, soul and mind that we enjoy them.

God of justice and truth, keep us faithful to our calling to be your people, even in the face of persecution or temptation, until that day when we drink the wine of the kingdom in your glorious presence. Amen

ESTHER'S FEAST

The king and Haman went in to feast with Queen Esther... [who said] 'If I have won your favour, O king... let my life be given me... and the lives of my people... For we have been sold... to be destroyed, to be killed, and to be annihilated. If we had been sold merely as slaves, men and women, I would have held my peace; but no enemy can compensate for this damage to the king.' Then King Ahasuerus said to Queen Esther, 'Who is he, and where is he, who has presumed to do this?' Esther said, 'A foe and enemy, this wicked Haman!' Then Haman was terrified before the king and the queen... Then Harbona... said, 'Look, the very gallows that Haman has prepared for Mordecai, whose word saved the king, stands at Haman's house, fifty cubits high.' And the king said, 'Hang him on that.' ...

Mordecai recorded these things, and sent letters to all the Jews... enjoining them that they should keep the fourteenth day of the month Adar and also the fifteenth day... as the days on which the Jews gained relief from their enemies, and as the month that had been turned for them from sorrow into gladness and from mourning into a holiday; that they should make them days of feasting and gladness, days for sending gifts of food to one another and presents to the poor.

ESTHER 7:1–6, 9; 9:20–22

While some Christians do not know much about Queen Esther, others find her story fascinating and inspiring. Although Jewish, of the tribe of Benjamin, she lived in Persia. Originally called Hadassah, which in Hebrew means 'myrtle', when she became queen she gained the Persian name Esther, which means 'star'.

While Esther is the star of the book that bears her name, Mordecai is her guardian cousin, who also has a semi-secret role as leader of the Jewish community in exile in the Persian city of Susa. King Ahasuerus is also known to history as Xerxes, and Esther is his second wife. She soon ingratiates herself by tipping him off about an assassination plot, and in this passage she informs him of a plot by one of his senior officials, Haman, to massacre Mordecai and the Jewish exiles. Xerxes pays attention and hoists Haman and his sons on his own 80-foot-high gallows. Consequently, the grateful Mordecai declares a festival—a period of feasting and generosity, to be celebrated yearly in early March. That festival still exists today and is known as Purim.

On Purim day, a festive meal is enjoyed, with plenty of wine. It is a jolly occasion and there is a saying in the Talmud (records of Jewish tradition dating between AD200 and 500) that one should drink on Purim until one cannot distinguish between *arur Haman* ('Cursed is Haman') and *baruch Mordechai* ('Blessed is Mordecai'). Some say that on Purim everything is allowed, although most Jewish leaders insist on decorum even in the midst of the merrymaking. Purim celebrates emotional reverse, from fasting to feasting, sadness to joy, terror to relief. Not only are food and wine consumed with gusto but gifts are exchanged and charitable donations made, a bit like Christmas for us.

Purim celebrates the way God's people were rescued by the careful intervention of a saviour figure. This reminds us of the saving work of Christ, operating on a much bigger, eternal scale. In Esther it is the Jews who are in danger. In reality, now, it is everyone who is in danger of the consequences of sin. The destruction of the Jews in Persia would have been the consequence of the sin of Haman, but the danger we all face is the consequence of our own sin.

Yet salvation from sin comes in and through Christ, who, through his intimate relationship with the Father, brings about rescue from the punishment for sin, which is death. And, in celebration of this saving work, Jesus, rather like Mordecai, gives us a feast to remember him by. For us too, sorrow turns to gladness and mourning to joy as we are liberated from the chains of sin. While the Jewish tradition has Purim, we have the feast of the Eucharist. In commemoration of his saving work, Christ gives us himself—'this is my body, this is my blood'—and we consciously remember and give thanks for this every time we eat the bread and take the cup. Since God the Father and Christ are united, it means that we not only thank God for Jesus' death and resurrection by which we are saved, but we also thank and remember Jesus himself.

There is something fundamentally religious in celebrating a festival, because it gives an opportunity to rejoice in the bountiful gifts of God, which we find not only in food but also in relationships, leisure, games and relaxation. These pleasures are also fundamentally human, so it is no surprise that festivals involve eating and drinking. We are built to want to give thanks and we are built to socialize, and, of course, we need to eat. So whether we are feasting at God's table in the presence of Christ or simply dining at home, let us always remember God's gifts, his generosity to us, not only in food and drink but in Jesus Christ.

Lord, when we celebrate your saving grace revealed in Christ, turn our sorrow into gladness and our sin into light. Amen

WEEK FOUR

MARY'S MAGNIFICAT

Mary said, 'My soul magnifies the Lord, and my spirit rejoices in God my Saviour, for he has looked with favour on the lowliness of his servant. Surely, from now on all generations will call me blessed; for the Mighty One has done great things for me, and holy is his name. His mercy is for those who fear him from generation to generation. He has shown strength with his arm; he has scattered the proud in the thoughts of their hearts. He has brought down the powerful from their thrones, and lifted up the lowly; he has filled the hungry with good things, and sent the rich away empty. He has helped his servant Israel, in remembrance of his mercy, according to the promise he made to our ancestors, to Abraham and to his descendants forever.'

LUKE 1:46–55

Mothering Sunday was the day when domestic servants were give time off to take their mothers a gift of simnel cake, a fruit cake made with eleven almond paste balls on top, representing the disciples (without Judas). Also known as *Laetare* (from the Latin *Laetare Jerusalem*—'Rejoice Jerusalem'—an ancient liturgical text for the day) or 'Refreshment Sunday', this can be considered a day on which Lenten abstinence is relaxed. Some traditions make this allowance for all Sundays in Lent, declaring them to be 'feast days' of the resurrection, thus leaving a 40-day Lent. On this middle Sunday of Lent there is a special focus on motherhood, and Mary the mother of Jesus is often remembered accordingly. So today is a good day on which to consider her great canticle of acceptance offered in response to the angel's promise that she would bear God's Son. In doing so, we move from the Old Testament to the New, a transition in which Mary herself is instrumental.

The Magnificat (meaning 'my soul magnifies' in Latin) is not about Mary but about God—his power, mercy and justice. She begins with a personal reflection concerning what God has done for her, and then she broadens her praise, including what God does for the poor and oppressed. In particular we notice the phrase 'he has filled the hungry with good things, and sent the rich away empty'. It is an inspiring thought, which has underscored much commitment to social justice and poverty alleviation. It seems that Mary is declaring that God has already dealt with these issues, but this is more of a vision of what we are called to attempt in God's name. As Teresa of Avila (1515–82) famously said, 'Christ has no body on earth but yours, no hands but yours, no feet but yours. Yours are the eyes through which Christ's compassion for the world is to look out; yours are the feet with which he is to go about doing good; and yours are the hands with which he is to bless us now.'

Yet we fall woefully short when it comes to food justice issues. While globalization has benefits, it can also be seen to aggravate injustice, engender racism, undermine health and cause hunger. The food on our plates often comes as a direct consequence of the discriminatory economic policies promulgated by rich nations who award themselves the capacity to call the tune and name the price. Subsidies or donations are often counterbalanced with loans or trade restrictions. As residents of wealthy nations, we are tainted by such policies and their effects, whether we like it or not.

Eating should promote fellowship, sharing, pleasure, delight and gratitude, and it often does, where 'grace' is prayed. So often, however, we neglect to give thanks and we ignore the questions of where food comes from and at what cost. Money aside, the cost is moral: the way we eat makes most Christians hypocrites, complacent about and complicit in economic and ethical behaviour that can be linked to pain, starvation and death.

It is not easy for most of us to break free or operate independently of society, and it is too easy to hide behind this fact. Buying fairly traded goods are a good start (although it is worth remembering that if those who are paid little lose their contracts, they end up with nothing). At the same time, we should not fall into the trap of assuming that we can take some relatively straightforward action which will get us out of this moral maze: we cannot save ourselves from sin, and trying to do so is blasphemous and futile.

It is God who heals, blesses, gives and forgives. Rather than trying to act to save ourselves from guilt or distancing ourselves from it, we should rather confess it. Individuals and societies that have lost sight of God's goodness manifest in the created order need to repent and confess their complicity in a global food system that is fundamentally unjust. It is good to remember that 'If we confess our sins, he who is faithful and just will forgive us our sins and cleanse us from all unrighteousness' (1 John 1:9). If we know this in our hearts and want to live the confession–absolution life that we profess, then we will act upon the confession we have made and the absolution we have received, and in that way begin to allow God to bring about change in and through us. Sin is followed by confession, which yields mercy, which inspires action. No other approach stands a chance in our tightly structured, unequal world.

Merciful God, we are inextricably bound by the sins of modern economics. Turn our hearts to confession, that we may be absolved and blessed to work for healing, justice and life for those who are oppressed by food injustice. Amen

HUMAN HUNGER

When Jesus saw the crowds, he went up the mountain; and after he sat down, his disciples came to him. Then he began to speak, and taught them, saying: 'Blessed are the poor in spirit, for theirs is the kingdom of heaven. Blessed are those who mourn, for they will be comforted. Blessed are the meek, for they will inherit the earth. Blessed are those who hunger and thirst for righteousness, for they will be filled. Blessed are the merciful, for they will receive mercy. Blessed are the pure in heart, for they will see God. Blessed are the peacemakers, for they will be called children of God. Blessed are those who are persecuted for righteousness' sake, for theirs is the kingdom of heaven.'

MATTHEW 5:1–10

We are born hungry. Before birth we are fed directly, but as soon as a baby becomes 'other', he or she has needs that must be met by others. Indeed, a baby has three basic needs: to eat, to sleep and to excrete. Lack of attendance to these basic animal functions causes discomfort and protest, as any parent knows. It is only after these needs are met that the serious human business of physical, mental and spiritual growth can properly begin. Only then can the experience of eating become a mutual one, in which our status as relational, dependent beings, limited by hunger and thirst, is lived out—except that in the wealthy West we are not accustomed to hunger. Our needs are generally met from the day we are born and, as babies, we soon let people know if we are hungry, tired or uncomfortable.

Consequently, most of us are never more hungry than the day we were born, and have no memory of it. Indeed, in our language, to be 'hungry' means something quite different from what it means to someone who is truly starving in a land where 'hunger' means that there is nothing to eat. Language changes, so we must be careful when we read biblical texts as we eat at our well-stocked dining tables. If we do not really know what the word 'hunger' means, we can easily misinterpret Jesus' words in the Sermon on the Mount, in which he speaks for those who 'hunger and thirst' for righteousness. Jesus is not speaking of desire for a meal or a thirst-quenching glass of water. Such hunger and thirst were no doubt felt in Jesus' time as they were now, but the possibility of real starvation underlies Jesus' comment.

In Jesus' time, many workers had no fixed employment and they would wait in the *agora* (the marketplace) to be hired for a day at a time. A day's wage was abut 4p in UK money, and was barely enough to live on. If they did not work they were not paid, and therefore they and their families could not eat. This is not a situation with which we are directly familiar but it is not so long ago that agricultural workers in Britain were in a similar position: no work meant no pay, so no food, which meant real hunger. This is the kind of scenario in which Jesus' parable of the labourers in the vineyard (Matthew 20:1–16) is set. Hence when Jesus speaks of hungering and thirsting, he not only means it but his hearers understand.

Before feeding the four thousand, Jesus said, 'I have compassion for the crowd, because they have been with me now for three days and have nothing to eat. If I send them away hungry to their homes, they will faint on the way—and some of them have come from a great distance' (Mark 8:2–3). That crowd had not eaten, and faced journeys home that might take hours or days. Being faint with hunger is something that those of us whose blood sugar drops fast will appreciate, but how many of us have gone for more than a day with nothing to eat? After three days, our bodies have used the energy from stored glucose so the liver begins to process body fat. After about three weeks, a genuine 'starvation mode' sets in as the body saps muscles and vital organs for energy. This can go on for over a month but eventually the damage becomes irreversible.

Jesus knew about this, not only because real hunger was a phenomenon of first-century life but because he fasted in the wilderness. He knew hunger and thirst and, difficult as it may be for us, we should think of the search for righteousness not in terms of a yen for a currant bun but in terms of a desperate, necessary craving for that which sustains us and prevents us from perishing. For without righteousness we are doomed, spiritually starved of that which saves us: the mercy, love and redemption of God, brought to the poor in spirit through Jesus Christ our Lord.

Father God, help us your children who may never have known true hunger to thirst after your righteousness and seek only you, that we may inherit your kingdom on earth and in heaven. Amen

GOOD AND BAD FRUIT

[Jesus said] 'In everything do to others as you would have them do to you; for this is the law and the prophets. Enter through the narrow gate; for the gate is wide and the road is easy that leads to destruction, and there are many who take it. For the gate is narrow and the road is hard that leads to life, and there are few who find it. Beware of false prophets, who come to you in sheep's clothing but inwardly are ravenous wolves. You will know them by their fruits. Are grapes gathered from thorns, or figs from thistles? In the same way, every good tree bears good fruit, but the bad tree bears bad fruit. A good tree cannot bear bad fruit, nor can a bad tree bear good fruit. Every tree that does not bear good fruit is cut down and thrown into the fire. Thus you will know them by their fruits.'
MATTHEW 7:12–20

There is an old joke about a man and his wife who go to heaven. On arrival they are shown around and are given a lovely house to live in, with sea views to one side, mountains to the other and a spacious, beautiful garden. When their tour is over, the woman says to the man, 'This is lovely. This truly is heaven.' Her husband replies, 'Yes, but just think, if we hadn't eaten all those fruit and vegetables we could have been here ages ago!'

We are often told these days that we should eat five portions of fruit and vegetables a day, in order to prevent cancers, strokes and heart disease and so live longer. Furthermore, fruits are full of vitamins, minerals, fibre and antidioxants and come in many different shapes, sizes and flavours, from avocado to grape, pomegranate to pineapple. The diversity of fruit mirrors the diversity of Christians. We are all entreated by Jesus and by Paul to search for and manifest the fruit of the Spirit. While Paul tells us that 'the fruit of the Spirit is love, joy, peace, patience, kindness, generosity, faithfulness, gentleness, and self-control' (Galatians 5:22–23), each of us has different gifts and, no doubt, a propensity to manifest different fruit according to our nature and calling.

Yet there is good fruit and bad fruit, as Jesus indicates in this passage from the Sermon on the Mount. He is speaking both spiritually and practically, for when he tells the outdoor congregation that the way to life involves passing through a narrow gate, and that they should strive to treat others as they would be treated in return, he is addressing their way of life. This ethical teaching is immediately followed by a warning against false prophets, whose lifestyle (their fruit) gives them away by the rottenness or inadequacy of what they yield.

Jesus' advice on how to recognize goodness and true faith in others is as accurate today as it was then. Indeed, the principle has found its way into many aspects of life, so that assessment, peer review and evaluation procedures are extremely common. Children, teachers, employees, managers, even clergy, are nowadays treated to various forms of 'review' by those who oversee them. The principle that underlies it all is the idea that the fruit of someone's labours can be assessed, evaluated, even quantified, so as to reveal that person's worth.

There is also a spiritual dimension to the fruit metaphor. Fruit in Jesus' time and place, as now, needed plenty of water. Barren trees yielded no fruit and soon withered, perhaps even dying. The incident in which Jesus cursed a fruitless fig tree reminds us of this fact (Matthew 21:18–22). Just as it is physically true that a tree without water bears no fruit, so it is with the fruit of faith, which must be nourished with the living water of the Spirit of Christ. In the life of faith, the spiritual and the physical combine when we think of fruit, for good spiritual fruit cannot be produced by a physically rotten tree: those who do not live according to Christ's law can hardly yield the fruit of love and peace and self-control.

The relationship between good works and spiritual fruit is similar to what biologists call a positive feedback loop, or cumulative causation: when a particular bodily chemical is needed (as in childbirth or injury), messages are sent causing its production, which itself yields not only an increase in the chemical required but also fresh stimulation to produce even more. So it is with the fruit of faith: those who live according to God's law will yield the fruit of the Spirit, which itself enables us to live by God's law and therefore yield even more fruit. A similar thing happens when we worship God, for in doing so we may receive the gift of the Spirit, who himself inspires, empowers and enables us to worship all the more authentically.

It is certainly healthy to eat fruit but, although doing so may well delay our demise, delaying the glories of eternity with God, it is even better to focus on producing fruit than on eating it. As followers of Christ, in word, deed and in spirit, we need to pay attention not only to the health of our bodies but also to the fruit of our faith, yielded each and every day.

Lord of heaven and earth, you bless us with fruit for healing and delight. May we, watered by the abundance of living water you pour upon us, bring forth the fruit of faith and life lived out according to your holy will. Amen

SIMON'S FISH

[Jesus] said to Simon, 'Put out into the deep water and let down your nets for a catch.' Simon answered, 'Master, we have worked all night long but have caught nothing. Yet if you say so, I will let down the nets.' When they had done this, they caught so many fish that their nets were beginning to break. So they signalled to their partners in the other boat to come and help them. And they came and filled both boats, so that they began to sink. But when Simon Peter saw it, he fell down at Jesus' knees, saying, 'Go away from me, Lord, for I am a sinful man!' For he and all who were with him were amazed at the catch of fish that they had taken; and so also were James and John, sons of Zebedee, who were partners with Simon. Then Jesus said to Simon, 'Do not be afraid; from now on you will be catching people.' When they had brought their boats to shore, they left everything and followed him.

LUKE 5:4-11

Have you seen the cartoon film *Happy Feet*? Ostensibly about a penguin called Mumble who cannot sing but tap dances instead, it tells of his journey to discover who are the 'aliens' who deplete the fish stocks of the southern seas, endangering the birds' survival. We are they, of course, whose exploitative greed damages food chains and wreaks havoc on environments.

The inspiration for the cartoon came from documentaries such as *March of the Penguins* and the BBC's *Planet Earth* series, which showed the remarkable endurance of Antarctica's Emperor penguins. First mothers, then fathers starve themselves for their young in a collaborative act of sacrificial suffering unparalleled in nature. The risks they take, travelling great distances away from the water to breed and huddling together to protect themselves and others from polar blizzards, are ultimately dependent on the reliability of food supplies, which human harvesting threatens. The consequences of inconsiderate fishing policies in that region are as obvious as they are inevitable.

Penguins are cute, of course, and their plight has captured the imagination of armchair ecologists. While this is a drop in the ocean as far as global warming and carbon emissions are concerned, it highlights the bigger issue about the number of fish in the sea and the interconnectedness of the life forms with which God has populated our blue and beautiful planet.

Thus it is ironic that in the story of the miraculous catch of fish, Simon Peter declares himself a sinner when he sees his bountiful haul. Those who haul ashore unsustainable catches of fish should perhaps express similar guilt and humility today. Simon's good fortune implies no guilt, however, but rather acknowledges God's gracious gift and his being an undeserving recipient of a miracle. Simon, here and later on, is aware of his own weakness and sin, which is why Jesus understands him, respects him and calls him into his service. Someone who is good and knows it does not make a good disciple or a good evangelist.

Simon, James and John had been fishing all night without luck (they were hardly at risk of depleting the fish stocks in the Sea of Galilee). The fish would have been sardines, which were prolific in the spring: as many as ten tons could be hauled on one outing. Once landed, the fish were soon grilled or fried or would be preserved by drying and salting. Gennesaret, the location of this episode, lay on the Sea of Galilee between Capernaum and Magdala, home to Mary, and its Greek name Taricheae means 'fish tower', where fish would have been strung up to be cured. Fish was a valuable commodity and Simon and his colleagues would have made a good living in that significant industry.

These fishermen take Jesus on board, who tells them (evidently with some authority) to fish on the other side of the boat, where a shoal must have been passing. Jesus' wisdom in this matter reveals his command over nature, his authority over others and his ability to bring about change not only in nature but in people. This miracle shares features with the changing of water into wine at Cana (John 2:1–10: see 'Jesus' wine', p. 115). Not only will Simon change into Peter, but he and James and John will be changed into fishers of people, through whom God in Christ will change the course of human and divine history.

Fish, when caught, becomes food, and when we eat food it becomes part of us. When a disciple helps someone to faith, by the grace of God they change not into food but into someone fed by the gospel. In bread and wine we 'eat' Christ, but there is a sense in which we are consumed by him as we become his body, the Church. By faith, God takes us into himself, welcoming us at the heavenly banquet of the kingdom, to dine at Christ's heavenly table of plenty, of mercy and of eternal resurrection life.

Heavenly Father, as you call us to witness to your love for all, make us aware of the delicate balances in creation, so that despite the sin of our greed and overconsumption, all your creatures may find redemption under the banner of that heavenly grace which you reveal in Jesus Christ our Lord. Amen

DAILY BREAD

[Jesus said] 'When you are praying, do not heap up empty phrases as the Gentiles do; for they think that they will be heard because of their many words. Do not be like them, for your Father knows what you need before you ask him. Pray then in this way: Our Father in heaven, hallowed be your name. Your kingdom come. Your will be done, on earth as it is in heaven. Give us this day our daily bread. And forgive us our debts, as we also have forgiven our debtors. And do not bring us to the time of trial, but rescue us from the evil one.'

MATTHEW 6:7–13

This passage is well known as the occasion on which Jesus teaches his disciples how to pray (in Luke 11:1–4 they specifically ask him to do so). Jesus teaches his disciples, and therefore us too, that we are to address God as 'our Father', not 'my father' or 'his father'. God is God of all, and when we pray we are partaking at a greater table of prayer, making our petitions as part of a spiritual community, yet all the while engaging with God on a personal and individual level. This is why, over the years, the saying of the Lord's Prayer together has become the *sine qua non* of corporate worship (it is hard to contemplate an Anglican wedding, funeral, baptism, Eucharist or special service that does not have everyone saying the Lord's Prayer together). Hence it has become known as the 'family' prayer: it is said together by the family of the church. It is also usable at home and that is partly why, until recently, we could assume that everyone would know the Lord's Prayer off by heart. The opening of the Eucharist service in the Book of Common Prayer requires the priest to say the Lord's Prayer aloud but alone, for this was not only a testimony of private devotion but also indicated to the congregation that the celebrant was, in fact, a properly authorized and educated priest who knew the Lord's Prayer.

At the same time, we are told to keep our relationship with God private, not to make a big show of it and to keep our prayer simple. Jesus' giving of the prayer is immediately followed by instruction on fasting, which brings into focus the elements of prayer that relate to the basic needs of life. Today we tend to interpret the request for 'daily bread' as being a reference to simple edible fare: we do not ask for fancy and copious amounts of food but only for what we need. Nor do we expect manna from heaven—food directly parachuted in by God—but rather desire the means and wherewithal to eat. In today's society, of course, that means money. Our 'daily bread' is the ability to go to the shops and buy enough food to feed ourselves, not lavishly but sufficiently. We also tend to extend the phrase into a metaphor, such that we are asking for the other basic necessities of life, such as clothes, warmth and shelter.

This is all very well, but we do not have the same understanding or experience of 'daily bread' as Christ's generation did. In first-century Palestine, 'bread' did not mean money or even food; it meant bread. Adam eats bread after being cast out of paradise (Genesis 3:19), and over time bread became not only the basic subsistence food but also the food kept in the house of God to signify the presence of the Lord (see Exodus 25:30). Only the priests were allowed to eat it and it was kept fresh, but on one occasion David and his men ate the bread of the presence because there was no alternative (1 Samuel 21:1–6). Jesus refers to this incident when he and his disciples are caught eating heads of wheat on the sabbath (Luke 6:1–5). The principle is one of satisfying need when resources are available, and the Lord's Prayer includes a petition that such resources may be available.

The making of bread was a painstaking task (see Ezekiel's recipe, p. 78), so we must also see the request for daily bread not only as referring to the resources to make bread. As Miriam Vamosh puts it, 'An understanding of the harsh physical labour associated with bread production gives us a greater appreciation of the famous words "Give us this day our daily bread" (Matt. 6:11). This was clearly not only a prayer for a good harvest or a means of purchasing the flour, but also an appeal for the stamina necessary to produce the bread.'[20]

At the heart of the Lord's Prayer is the request for daily bread, and that implies daily prayer. Each day we need food, and we ask for it and our Lord provides. Let us never forget to ask for our daily bread or take it for granted, but may we pray as the family of God that our needs may be met, to his glory.

Praise be to you, O God, who hears prayer and gives us the daily resources to live and pray and witness to your loving kindness. Amen

FISH AND BREAD FOR FIVE THOUSAND

Now the Passover, the festival of the Jews, was near. When he looked up and saw a large crowd coming towards him, Jesus said to Philip, 'Where are we to buy bread for these people to eat?' He said this to test him, for he himself knew what he was going to do. Philip answered him, 'Six months' wages would not buy enough bread for each of them to get a little.' One of his disciples, Andrew, Simon Peter's brother, said to him, 'There is a boy here who has five barley loaves and two fish. But what are they among so many people?' Jesus said, 'Make the people sit down.' Now there was a great deal of grass in the place; so they sat down, about five thousand in all. Then Jesus took the loaves, and when he had given thanks, he distributed them to those who were seated; so also the fish, as much as they wanted. When they were satisfied, he told his disciples, 'Gather up the fragments left over, so that nothing may be lost.' So they gathered them up, and from the fragments of the five barley loaves, left by those who had eaten, they filled twelve baskets.

JOHN 6:4–13

Do you ever attend 'bring and share' meals? They have advantages when catering for large numbers: many hands make light work if each person brings something. The cost is rarely great, and people need spend only what they can afford. Some people prepare home-cooked dishes while others bring something from a shop, depending on their talents, time constraints and financial capacity. Each approach is valid and valued, and so at a common table everyone is equal yet different—a good model for the kingdom of heaven. More importantly, these meals embody the idea of sharing, such that you do not necessarily eat what you prepared, and you enjoy what others bring. Some coordination is needed so that a group doesn't end up with 30 puddings and two quiches.

This model of hospitality reminds us not only of the feeding of the five thousand but also of the practices of the early Church. When the first Christians met on the 'Lord's Day' (the first day of the week, the day after the sabbath), they ate together, and in the context of a shared meal they celebrated what we may consider to be the first Eucharists. One of the earliest examples of a Communion liturgy, attributed to Hippolytus of Rome (c.160–235), involves not only bread and wine but olives and milk, and represents the transition from a communal meal to an act of worship. Yet when Paul wrote to the Corinthian churches, around AD60, he rebuked them for not 'sharing' properly: 'each of you goes ahead with your own supper, and one goes hungry and another becomes drunk' (1 Corinthians 11:21). Paul reminds us that it is in the spirit of sharing—not only that we share with each other but also that Christ shares himself with us in bread and wine—that we join together as one large family, partaking of food, of Christ and of each other's gifts, talents and personalities. Thus, in one of many senses, we become and behave as the body of Christ, and that is a kind of miracle, enacted in us whenever we join together as Christian communities in table fellowship and worship.

'Bring and share' lies at the heart of the feeding of the five thousand and its partner miracle, the feeding of the four thousand, in which fewer are fed with slightly more bread (Matthew 15:32–38). As a consequence of a willingness to share resources and trust in God, everyone is satisfied. When it is put as simply as that, we might well wonder about our own national and international unwillingness to share resources and trust each other and God. Yesterday we looked at the Lord's Prayer and its daily appeal for bread. Prayer is important for spiritual sustenance but bread is equally important for physical renewal. Part of Christ's call to us is to pray and worship God and also to provide the hungry with bread. Tomorrow we will encounter Jesus as the 'bread of life', in a passage that follows this one. We must connect them and realize that, as Jesus provides physical bread for the five thousand, he also provides himself as spiritual sustenance yielding physical resurrection.

John tells us that this feeding miracle takes place at Passover—a key theme for John, who emphasizes Jesus as the new Passover lamb, slain for all people as redemption is made available for all. John also tells us (in the original Greek) that the five thousand are all men, and that they are made to sit down in the spring grass. Hidden in the detail that they are men may be a reference to the fact that they are zealous Jews, hoping that Jesus will become a revolutionary Messiah. While they are fed, the miracle is also a sign that Jesus is not their kind of messiah, offering masculine, militaristic insurrection, but is a spiritual light and doorway to resurrection for those who feed on the bread of life.

Christ, light of the world, you illuminate our souls with the mercy of God and feed our hearts with the food of love; by your Holy Spirit, lead us day by day into your Father's presence. Amen

LIFE'S BREAD

'Our ancestors ate the manna in the wilderness; as it is written, "He gave them bread from heaven to eat."' Then Jesus said to them, 'Very truly, I tell you, it was not Moses who gave you the bread from heaven, but it is my Father who gives you the true bread from heaven. For the bread of God is that which comes down from heaven and gives life to the world.' They said to him, 'Sir, give us this bread always.' Jesus said to them, 'I am the bread of life. Whoever comes to me will never be hungry, and whoever believes in me will never be thirsty... Your ancestors ate the manna in the wilderness, and they died. This is the bread that comes down from heaven, so that one may eat of it and not die. I am the living bread that came down from heaven. Whoever eats of this bread will live for ever; and the bread that I will give for the life of the world is my flesh.'
JOHN 6:31–35, 49–51

When I typed the word 'bread' into a supermarket website search engine, it offered me a choice of 100 kinds of bread. White, brown, wholemeal, sliced, unsliced—the choice is extensive. In Jesus' day there was much less variety: there were two basic kinds of bread, barley bread and whiter wheat-based bread. The former was the bread of the people. It was coarse, often very hard, but cheaper and more readily available than softer white bread. Earlier in John's Gospel, in the account of the feeding of the five thousand, Andrew tells Jesus that there is a boy with 'five barley loaves' (6:9). Barley bread was the kind of bread eaten by the people who followed Jesus. The bread echoed their lives—hard and common. Wheat bread was for the rich. When Jesus says, 'I am the bread of life', we should think of coarse barley bread, not of nice sliced white from a supermarket aisle.

In Luke's account of the birth of Jesus, we are told three times that he was placed in a manger in Bethlehem (2:7, 12, 16). This fact (the key to every Sunday school nativity play) helps us to notice that Christ, the Son of God, is sent as food for the world, making his first appearance in human form in a food trough in a town called 'Bethlehem', which literally means 'house of bread'. When we encounter Jesus describing himself as 'the bread of life' in John's Gospel, we should remember this. We might also remember Jesus saying a little later, 'The Father and I are one' (10:30), for we can see how God's understanding of Christ is the same as Jesus' understanding of himself. Bound into this self-understanding that Father and Son have is the idea that Christ comes as spiritual nourishment for a world that has been starved of salvation. Christ is born into a dark world of sin and offers himself not only as a sacrifice for sin but as metaphorical food. Once we realize this, we can see that the metaphor continues throughout the Gospels, from birth in a manger through various miracles and sayings, right up to the final eucharistic Passover meal at which Jesus declares, 'This is my body, which is given for you' (Luke 22:19). Then, as the story continues into the light of resurrection, we meet travellers on the road to Emmaus, to whom Jesus is revealed 'in the breaking of the bread' (Luke 24:35), and we finally see Peter reconciled at a breakfast with Christ on a beach (John 21).

Generally, Christians see the passion of Christ and the Eucharist as both pointing towards and recalling for us his suffering, through which he redeemed and saved the world. Theologians speak of 'penal substitution' and 'atonement', such that Christ is seen as 'taking our place', 'bearing our sins' and 'paying the price'. Some people find this doctrine unhelpful because it hints at a vengeful God, who has to punish somebody and so punishes his own Son instead of us. God is not satisfied, it might seem, without blood, pain and sacrifice. This is but one dimension of the vast victory that Christ won on the cross for us and our salvation, and it is not something that he simply did and for which we just say 'yes' and 'thank you'. We are involved in his offering of himself; we need to take it into ourselves, own it—ingest it, almost. And that is where the idea of Christ as 'food' can be helpful. That is why we find it embedded into New Testament scripture, sometimes so deep that we hardly notice it. The Eucharist is not just a remembering or a re-enactment, as some believe, but it is a consuming. We consume bread and wine in a symbolic meal and, in doing so, we are consumed into the faith of Jesus, who not only died for us but lives for us as the bread of life, now and into eternity. Jesus says it himself: 'I am the living bread that came down from heaven. Whoever eats of this bread will live for ever; and the bread that I will give for the life of the world is my flesh' (John 6.51).

Jesus Christ, bread of heaven, as we are consumed by your loving redemption, feed us now and evermore. Amen

WEEK FIVE

EUCHARISTIC FOOD

The Jews then disputed among themselves, saying, 'How can this man give us his flesh to eat?' So Jesus said to them, 'Very truly, I tell you, unless you eat the flesh of the Son of Man and drink his blood, you have no life in you. Those who eat my flesh and drink my blood have eternal life, and I will raise them up on the last day; for my flesh is true food and my blood is true drink. Those who eat my flesh and drink my blood abide in me, and I in them. Just as the living Father sent me, and I live because of the Father, so whoever eats me will live because of me. This is the bread that came down from heaven, not like that which your ancestors ate, and they died. But the one who eats this bread will live for ever.'
JOHN 6:52–58

These days, we tend to be sceptical about spiritual symbolism and, unless we are attached to a Roman Catholic eucharistic doctrine, we may be wary of questions about what the bread and wine of Communion really are. This has been debated much over the centuries. Thomas Aquinas (c.1225–74) contributed significantly to the thinking about what happens to bread and wine when consecrated by a priest. His main view is described as 'transubstantiation', whereby the appearance of bread and wine remain unchanged by priestly consecration but their real essence is miraculously converted into the body and blood of Christ, who is therefore truly present in Communion. Aquinas' ideas are still very much alive in Roman Catholic doctrine, although they were strongly rejected by reformers such as Calvin, Luther, Zwingli and Cranmer, who thought this idea too mystical and priest-centred and preferred to focus on the dimensions of memorial and gratitude in the Eucharist. The question of what the bread and wine *becomes* has influenced modern history irrevocably, because it fuelled reformations and counter-reformations of churches which produced a steady flow of martyrs on both sides. The idea that the status of the meal of remembrance recalling the sacrifice that Christ made for us should itself become a wound in history, the scars of which are very much still with us, is ironic indeed.

The sacrifice of Christ and his being the bread of life are interconnected. The act of remembrance comes through eating. We may not always remember what we eat but in Christ we eat what we remember. On one level, the transformation of bread to body and wine to blood is of little consequence, for the bread and wine do not need to be seen as 'changing' at all. If we read John 6 carefully, we realize that the bread is Jesus in the first place. Jesus associates himself with the commonest form of food—simple bread, without which people starved. So in Jesus' association of himself with bread, there are both physical and spiritual dimensions.

First, Jesus is like a substance of simplicity and necessity. He is a basic need, and without him, without 'eating' him, we starve spiritually. Without him, in fact, we also starve physically. The Anglican Communion service contains those apposite words, 'All things come from you and of your own do we give you.' This reminds us that all bread—all food—comes from God. Whether we remember the story in Genesis in which God gives food to creation (Genesis 1:29–30) or logically conclude that if everything comes from our Creator God then that must include our food, there is a sense in which Christ as the bread of life is true physically as well as spiritually. Christ, at one with God, is literally the provider. He provides food for both physical and spiritual survival, but he also declares that he is that food. Before his birth, before the feeding miracles recorded in the Bible and before the last supper, Christ is both Word and Bread. Both are crucial for salvation; indeed, they are the same thing. Thus questions about when the bread of Communion 'becomes' Christ seem a little odd. Christ is the bread of life and always has been. There is a sense in which the bread of Communion is the body of Christ before we start our prayers.

A few hundred years ago, I might have been burned at the stake for writing that previous sentence. We have come a long way since then but Christ has not changed. When we eat bread, we eat physical salvation, and when we eat Communion we eat spiritual salvation. In eating, we take it into ourselves, and it becomes part of us and we part of it. The physical and spiritual are inseparable, even before we 'celebrate Communion' and remember the sacrifice Christ made in dying and rising again for us. And that dying and rising again makes no sense unless we understand Christ as food, readily and gratefully partaking in the generous banquet of himself to which he invites us.

Lord Jesus Christ, Word of God, you became human and offered yourself as spiritual food so that we might come to know you in your physical resurrection. Be for us a real presence in our lives until we dine with you at your heavenly banquet, where you live and reign with the Father and the Spirit. Amen

JESUS' WINE

On the third day there was a wedding in Cana of Galilee, and the mother of Jesus was there. Jesus and his disciples had also been invited to the wedding. When the wine gave out, the mother of Jesus said to him, 'They have no wine.' And Jesus said to her, 'Woman, what concern is that to you and to me? My hour has not yet come.' His mother said to the servants, 'Do whatever he tells you.' Now standing there were six stone water-jars for the Jewish rites of purification, each holding twenty or thirty gallons. Jesus said to them, 'Fill the jars with water.' And they filled them up to the brim. He said to them, 'Now draw some out, and take it to the chief steward.' So they took it. When the steward tasted the water that had become wine, and did not know where it came from (though the servants who had drawn the water knew), the steward called the bridegroom and said to him, 'Everyone serves the good wine first, and then the inferior wine after the guests have become drunk. But you have kept the good wine until now.'

JOHN 2:1–10

Although this story appears to be about marriage—'which holy estate Christ adorned and beautified with his presence, and first miracle that he wrought, in Cana of Galilee' (Book of Common Prayer)—it is also significant because it reveals something about first-century parties. But it is most important because it is all about change.

The story begins with Jesus, an invited guest, attending, supporting and loving those whose big day it is. In what seems to us a remarkable twist, the wine runs out, which would have caused considerable embarrassment to any host. Jesus doesn't want to get involved (he is not simply a miracle worker, even if that is what Mary wants), but he accedes to his mother's desire, directing the servants to fill the foot-washing jars. Mary and Jesus must have had considerable influence (or been very close friends of the family) for the servants to do this, but it is excellent advice, as the wine that materializes turns out to be 'good' wine.

Good wine meant wine in which the amount of exposure to air had been well judged. The carbon dioxide produced as the sugar in the grape juice ferments is forced to the surface, which bubbles. The carbon dioxide must be allowed to escape but there is a risk that the exposed liquid will be contaminated by fungus, which turns the wine into vinegar. In biblical times, resin from the terebinth tree was sometimes used to prevent this chemical reaction from spoiling the wine. The wine that Jesus produced was 'good'—better than the wine that had already been served, which, like much poor wine of that period, was pretty close to vinegar. It seems it was the best that the host had to hand (indeed, it was all he had).

While it was conventional to dilute wine, the water in the jars was not intended for this purpose but for holding the water used to wash people's feet. And just as he changed water into wine, so Jesus is going to change people. He is going to change ordinary people like you and me into the greatest vintages in the kingdom of heaven. In John's Gospel, this story is the first major event in Jesus' ministry of healing, preaching and change. That ministry begins at his baptism, when Jesus is drawn into a different kind of relationship with everyone around him. Just as the baptism involved water, so too does this first miracle. John also points us forward to the wine of the Passover cups, one of which Jesus describes as his blood. The water at Cana is turned into good wine, the good wine of Eucharist—the wine that we still share today, the wine of the kingdom. It is the wine of Jesus' blood, which began as water and ends as blood, where water signifies life and blood death.

This rich story resonates with biblical history, in which wine making and drinking was a fundamental dimension of human existence (see 'Noah gets drunk', p. 30, and 'Isaiah's vineyard', p. 68), but it also speaks to us today about the power of God by whom we are changed, and about the miracles that happen around us almost unnoticed. The American statesman and scientist Benjamin Franklin wrote to his friend, the French economist Andre Morellet in 1779, 'We hear of... water into wine... as a miracle. But this conversion is, through the goodness of God, made every day before our eyes. Behold the rain which descends from heaven upon our vineyards, and which incorporates itself with the grapes, to be changed into wine: a constant proof that God loves us and wants us to be happy.'[21]

Happiness is something that many would say is induced by wine (see Psalm 104:15), but a greater happiness is to be found in following Christ, in whom and by whom we are changed as we move through our imperfect lives.

Changeless Christ, whose saving blood has become the wine of the eternal kingdom, may we grow to become more and more like you as you change us from glory to glory. Amen

LIVING WATER

Now the Jewish festival of Booths was near... [Jesus] also went, not publicly but as it were in secret... About the middle of the festival Jesus went up into the temple and began to teach. The Jews were astonished at it, saying, 'How does this man have such learning, when he has never been taught?' ... Jesus cried out as he was teaching in the temple, 'You know me, and you know where I am from. I have not come on my own. But the one who sent me is true, and you do not know him... On the last day of the festival, the great day, while Jesus was standing there, he cried out, 'Let anyone who is thirsty come to me, and let the one who believes in me drink. As the scripture has said, "Out of the believer's heart shall flow rivers of living water."' Now he said this about the Spirit, which believers in him were to receive; for as yet there was no Spirit, because Jesus was not yet glorified.

JOHN 7:2, 10, 14–15, 28, 37–39 (ABRIDGED)

Water is the simplest form of drink: it contains no calories and few minerals or vitamins, but we are largely made of water and without it we die. Even those who fast must take water. Water is the juice of life; it is the liquid of baptism, the rain from heaven, and it covers two thirds of the earth's surface. We know it as ice caps, oceans and geysers and, while we depend on it, it is water that may ultimately inundate and destroy our habitat. We are told that global warming and carbon emissions will eventually cause ice caps to melt, sea levels to rise and large populated areas to be submerged. Many places, such as Bangladesh, already face this fear today, and disaster could be widespread should the delicate balances of temperature and sea level be even slightly altered. The sea is one of the most powerful forces known to us: we can hardly control it and yet without it we would not exist.

Water nourishes the earth and it is no surprise that ancient Jewish culture recognized, celebrated and gave thanks for it. Harvest festivals, whether celebrated in churches today or the villages of the ancient Middle East, are expressions of praise and thanksgiving, at least in part for the gift of water to promote and sustain agricultural growth. There was a Jewish festival, the Feast of Tabernacles (or 'Booths', *succoth* in Hebrew), which was an early version of harvest festival: 'You shall keep the festival of booths for seven days, when you have gathered in the produce from your threshing-floor and your wine press... for the Lord your God will bless you in all your produce and in all your undertakings, and you shall surely celebrate' (Deuteronomy 16:13, 15).

The seventh day of the Festival of Booths culminated in a particular ritual involving water. The people gathered in and around the temple mount in Jerusalem and the priests would pour water down the mount, streams of water celebrating the gift of life and the abundance of God's goodness. This flowing water was also reminiscent of the water that Moses produced from the rock at Horeb (Exodus 17:6). It is extremely likely that this very act was taking place when Jesus invited the crowd to come to him for living water. In his Gospel, John has already quoted Jesus saying to the Samaritan woman, 'Those who drink of the water that I will give them will never be thirsty. The water that I will give will become in them a spring of water gushing up to eternal life' (4:14). Now he portrays Jesus saying a similar thing with the most amazing visual aid occurring behind him. Similarly to the way in which he likens himself to the Passover lamb, Jesus associates his mission and ministry with another Jewish tradition, the flowing water of the feast of Tabernacles. It is as though he says, 'You see the water flowing down the mountain? That is me. I am the living water and, if you drink of me, you will never thirst.'

John tells us that he is referring to the gift of the Holy Spirit, yet to be given but imminent. Not only is Jesus going to give living water but the water is going to flow out as well as in; the Spirit will gush forth from those who have drunk of Christ, spreading the love and mercy of God until the end of the age.

While we all need water, most of us do not drink enough of it. In some parts of the world people cannot, because it is scarce, while we who can simply turn on a tap may still not drink the two litres a day that some doctors recommend. The Holy Spirit is often likened to water—flowing, gushing, baptizing, even drowning us. Many people do not seek much of that Spirit, surviving on the minimum, while others seem to have none, dwelling in a spiritual desert lacking faith and denying divine love. Yet God's gift of the Spirit causes our cup to overflow (Psalm 23:5), and truly we cannot have too much of him.

God, who in Christ blesses the earth with the living water of your Spirit, fill us until we overflow with that living water of your love and mercy, to cleanse, revive and refresh our barren world. Amen

THE HEAVENLY BANQUET

[Jesus said] 'The kingdom of heaven may be compared to a king who gave a wedding banquet for his son. He sent his slaves to call those who had been invited to the wedding banquet, but they would not come. Again he sent other slaves, saying, "Tell those who have been invited: Look, I have prepared my dinner, my oxen and my fat calves have been slaughtered, and everything is ready; come to the wedding banquet." But they made light of it and went away, one to his farm, another to his business, while the rest seized his slaves, maltreated them, and killed them. The king was enraged. He sent his troops, destroyed those murderers, and burned their city. Then he said to his slaves, "The wedding is ready, but those invited were not worthy. Go therefore into the main streets, and invite everyone you find to the wedding banquet." Those slaves went out into the streets and gathered all whom they found, both good and bad; so the wedding hall was filled with guests.

'But when the king came in to see the guests, he noticed a man there who was not wearing a wedding robe, and he said to him, "Friend, how did you get in here without a wedding robe?" And he was speechless. Then the king said to the attendants, "Bind him hand and foot, and throw him into the outer darkness, where there will be weeping and gnashing of teeth." For many are called, but few are chosen.'

MATTHEW 22:2–14

In my role as Honorary Chaplain to the Worshipful Company of Cordwainers, I am regularly called upon to say grace both at small suppers and at great dinners. The Cordwainers, like many London Livery Companies and Guilds, date back to medieval London, where they were responsible for the oversight of the shoemaking profession ('cordwain' refers to the leather imported from Cordoba, Spain, which was used for making shoes). There are four key factors that still relate to Liveries and Guilds today. Firstly, they are often 'Worshipful Companies', which means that they have a Christian foundation, and prayer and worship still lie at the heart of what they do. No meeting or meal begins without prayer and thanksgiving to God. Secondly, they still take a charitable and benevolent interest in the trades they represent today. Thirdly, to varying degrees, past liverymen and benefactors have endowed them with historic wealth, which, fourthly, is mostly used for charitable causes. I heard it said recently that London Livery Companies give more to charity than does the National Lottery.

In hospitality, relationships are cemented, care shared and minds expanded. The wider family of the host organization gather together to remind themselves who they are and what their purpose is, and they also extend welcome and favour towards their guests. The event closest to this kind of meal, that many of us experience, is a wedding banquet, at which many are invited to eat together and celebrate a marriage.

Livery dinners, college feasts, state banquets and wedding receptions may be the closest we now have to the kind of occasion Jesus is thinking of when he describes the wedding banquet to which God invites us. The parable is not simply about a banquet at which everyone dines well and has a good time, although this is what many people derive from the analogy. It is actually a parable about judgment, in which those who are invited (the Jewish Pharisees and scribes) decline. Having thrown open the doors to all comers, in what looks like a wonderful gesture of impartial hospitality (as embodied in Luke 14:8–13, in which Jesus instructs his disciples not to take the highest place or honour and to invite those who cannot repay the favour), the host then expels an undesirable, whom he addresses as 'friend'. This parable presents us not with universal hospitality but with universal invitation.

Continued presence at the banquet is not determined by status, yet there are criteria for remaining welcome: we must have a wedding robe. That is to say, we must be clothed in righteousness and salvation. Paul describes the cloth of the wedding banquet robe when he writes, 'As God's chosen ones, holy and beloved, clothe yourselves with compassion, kindness, humility, meekness, and patience... Above all, clothe yourselves with love, which binds everything together in perfect harmony' (Colossians 3:12, 14). This is good advice whether we dine simply at home with friends and family, enjoy banquets or eat alone in front of the television. In any event, we are called to be compassionate, kind, humble, patient and loving, not only in hospitality but in everything we do. If we model ourselves on this, then by the grace of God we too will come to dine at that heavenly banquet with all the saints: '"Let us rejoice and exult and give him the glory, for the marriage of the Lamb has come, and his bride has made herself ready; to her it has been granted to be clothed with fine linen, bright and pure"—for the fine linen is the righteous deeds of the saints' (Revelation 19:7–8).

Christ our bridegroom, as we anticipate the heavenly banquet prepared for your faithful people, fashion us according to your will, that we may wear the wedding robes of salvation and dine with you for ever. Amen

CHRIST'S SYMPOSIUM

Then Levi gave a great banquet for him in his house; and there was a large crowd of tax-collectors and others sitting at the table with them. The Pharisees and their scribes were complaining to his disciples, saying, 'Why do you eat and drink with tax-collectors and sinners?' Jesus answered, 'Those who are well have no need of a physician, but those who are sick; I have come to call not the righteous but sinners to repentance.' Then they said to him, 'John's disciples, like the disciples of the Pharisees, frequently fast and pray, but your disciples eat and drink.' Jesus said to them, 'You cannot make wedding guests fast while the bridegroom is with them, can you? The days will come when the bridegroom will be taken away from them, and then they will fast in those days.'

LUKE 5:29–35

When the Church of England trains people for ministry as priests and deacons, there are various subjects that ordinands must study. For some, this may feel a bit like hoop-jumping, as classes are attended, assignments written and placements in different churches undertaken. But there is another dimension of theological education which is very important, but is often taken for granted, and that is fellowship at meal times. Dining together is not only a sociable thing to do, it is also an experience through which relationships are formed and learning takes place. Meals invariably involve conversation, and conversation involves listening, which leads to empathy, challenge and change.

What we forget in today's context is that eating and learning together have always gone hand in hand. The colleges of Oxford and

Cambridge and other ancient universities were built around a chapel and a dining hall: food and prayer lay at the heart of the academic community and, to some extent, still do today. If we travel further into the past, we find scholars dining in what became known as a symposium. The word is still used today but in a limited sense of its full meaning. In classical Greek culture, a symposium was a meal at which the diners reclined on couches while eating and drinking. Conversation, discussion, even heated argument were integral parts of a symposium, which literally means 'drinking with'.

One of the most famous accounts of a symposium was composed by Plato, whose *Symposium* purports to recreate dialogues on the subject of love which took place at a drinking party hosted by Agathon in Athens around 416BC. Among the guests who speak are Socrates and the playwright Alcibiades. As well as lively debate, we learn of their petty jealousies, how they recline on couches together and ultimately how they disperse when a group of drunks turn up.

It is not so far away from the idea of gentlemen retiring from the dinner table to smoke, talk and drink port, although there is evidence that in Greco-Roman culture women were often present at symposia. The diners would recline, and, typically, there were three people on each of three couches. The most important people would recline on the central couch, often with one of them presiding over the discussion (and deciding how diluted the wine should be). Thus, symposia were rather like academic seminars, at which students and staff also ate and drank, sometimes to excess. It was also customary to recline to eat in Babylonian, Roman and Jewish cultures.

When we read of Jesus dining with people such as Levi or Zacchaeus (Luke 19:1–10), we must appreciate the teaching opportunities that these meals afforded. Levi invites Jesus to a symposium in his house and, after Zaccheus has decided to follow him, Jesus invites himself to his house, not simply to eat but to teach. The Pharisees clearly do not like this kind of thing: they think that Jesus should not go near these impromptu symposia at which food is eaten, wine is drunk and discussion arises. Their opinion is that Jesus and his entourage should fast in the face of such festivities, setting a good example, as they believe they and the disciples of John the Baptist do. They would rather retreat to a moralistic high ground than join in. But such a high ground is remote and barren and there is nothing to be achieved by being there, Jesus seems to say.

Some people suggest that if Jesus were with us today, he would be evangelizing in pubs and bars, and in a sense that is what he was doing at the dining parties that Luke is so fond of describing. As Robert J. Karris puts it, 'In Luke's gospel, Jesus is either going to a meal, at a meal, or coming home from a meal... Jesus got himself killed because of the way he ate.'[22] Jesus did not care what the scribes and Pharisees thought of his actions or his methods of teaching: the end (the kingdom of God) justified the means (symposium-style encounters). Jesus met sinners and tax collectors on their home territory and made it his own. This is a challenging fact, worth remembering in this and every age of mission and evangelism.

Lord of every place, preside over all our meals as teacher, judge and friend. Guide us and give us courage to dine with strangers and share with them your gospel of reconciliation, mercy and peace. Amen

THE CANAANITE WOMAN'S PLEA

Jesus left that place and went away to the district of Tyre and Sidon. Just then a Canaanite woman from that region came out and started shouting, 'Have mercy on me, Lord, Son of David; my daughter is tormented by a demon.' But he did not answer her at all. And his disciples came and urged him, saying, 'Send her away, for she keeps shouting after us.' He answered, 'I was sent only to the lost sheep of the house of Israel.' But she came and knelt before him, saying, 'Lord, help me.' He answered, 'It is not fair to take the children's food and throw it to the dogs.' She said, 'Yes, Lord, yet even the dogs eat the crumbs that fall from their masters' table.' Then Jesus answered her, 'Woman, great is your faith! Let it be done for you as you wish.' And her daughter was healed instantly.

MATTHEW 15:21–28

The television news journalist Rageh Omar, who reported for the BBC from Iraq throughout the war of 2003, made a three-part TV series about the miracles of Jesus. Omar, who was raised a Muslim, takes a dispassionate view of the Gospel material, not asking whether Jesus' miracles occurred or not but rather examining their impact upon and meaning for those who were present at the time. The series has been released by Bible Society on a DVD with study notes for schools and church groups to use.[23] In the programmes, Omar devotes several minutes to this story of the Canaanite woman and he considers what her encounter with Jesus meant for those present.

While Jesus and his disciples were Jewish, she was not. She and we are cruelly reminded of that fact in this encounter when Jesus refers to 'dogs', a disparaging and common slang word used by Jews to refer to Gentiles. In using the word in front of his disciples, Jesus is apparently aligning himself with what was probably a conventional but racist attitude. It is something of a test for the woman, and also for his disciples. They would have baulked at associating with non-Jews, who, like dogs, were considered dirty. The woman evidently passes the test, for she gets her heart's desire—healing for her daughter. She refuses to be humiliated in the face of an old-fashioned, misogynistic and racist tradition, yet the fact that she approaches Jesus at all reveals that she hopes for, even expects, more of him than predictable rejection. And of course, she is right. She gets her miracle, and those who look on in disgust get a sign—a sign of a new order in which the kingdom is opened to everyone, as the healing grace of God is extended in every direction.

In spite of the reference to breadcrumbs in this story, it is not about food but about salvation. We must not overlook the imagery, however. Jesus, who referred to himself as the 'bread of life' and described the Passover bread as his very own body, uses food imagery to powerful effect here. While the reference to dogs is a symptom of the old way of thinking, the self-reference to bread is a sign of the new. So even in questioning her right to ask for bread (God's healing grace), Jesus indicates that it is possible for her to have some. In humility she approaches Christ, who is grace incarnate, and she seeks bread—spiritual food by which she and her daughter can be fed and freed.

In the light of this aspect of a humble but expectant person approaching the throne of grace, Archbishop Cranmer introduced what we call the 'prayer of humble access' into the Communion liturgy in 1548. Anglicans are still familiar with the prayer, which begins, 'We do not presume to come to this your table, merciful Lord' and contains the words 'We are not worthy so much as to gather up the crumbs from under your table, but you are the same Lord, whose nature is always to have mercy'. This prayer turns the Canaanite woman's experience into our experience and reminds us that we, like her, are not automatically recipients of mercy and love. Indeed, we are dirty sinners, who can barely expect even divine scraps of grace. Yet God, in his infinite love and mercy, through Christ's death and resurrection, offers not scraps but a heavenly banquet to all who approach in humility and penitence.

While we have the assurance of mercy given in word and sacrament, it is appropriate to be humble before God. That is why the prayer of humble access is so apt, and that is why the story of the Canaanite woman, in which acceptance overrules rejection, is so important to those of us whose spiritual heritage is basically Gentile in origin. Now the bread of heaven is made available to us all because of the liberating work of Jesus, the bread of life.

Mysterious and merciful Christ, you confound us with your words and actions. We thank you for the privilege of being your people and for the access to the Father that you make possible. By your Spirit, make us humble sharers of your bread for the world until that day when every barrier of race and gender is broken down in your eternal kingdom. Amen

---

LAZARUS' SABBATH SUPPER

Six days before the Passover Jesus came to Bethany, the home of Lazarus, whom he had raised from the dead. There they gave a dinner for him. Martha served, and Lazarus was one of those at the table with him… When the great crowd of the Jews learned that he was there, they came not only because of Jesus but also to see Lazarus, whom he had raised from the dead. So the chief priests planned to put Lazarus to death as well, since it was on account of him that many of the Jews were deserting and were believing in Jesus.

JOHN 12:1–2, 9–11

When Matthew, Mark and Luke tell us about Jesus' 'triumphal' entry into Jerusalem, they do not specifically remind us, as John does, that the Passover was approaching. As we shall see, John has a particular interest in the Passover, wanting to emphasize Jesus as the 'Lamb of God'. As we approach the final week of Lent, we are in the midst of Passiontide and we are beginning Holy Week. But Holy Week is also the run-up to Passover, and what we call Palm Sunday—tomorrow— was the day after the final sabbath before the Passover.

The sabbath before Passover has various traditions connected with it, many of which are still celebrated today. Known as *Shabbat Hagadol*, Jewish tradition associates this day with the preparations that the Israelites made in Egypt before the first Passover, when the firstborn males in Egypt were to be killed by plague (Exodus 12; see p. 46). The date on which they were given instructions for the Passover was the 'tenth of the month', and the Passover itself came five days later. Tradition has it that once the lambs were selected, they were tied to the bedposts in Jewish homes for safe-keeping. Inevitably this behaviour was noticed by the Egyptians, who also knew that livestock trading and other work was forbidden on a sabbath. So they asked the Israelites what they were doing and were told of God's plans to slay the firstborn (because it was a sabbath, the Israelites were forbidden from being dishonest about their plans). Some Egyptians then demanded of Pharaoh that he let the Israelites go, but he refused and there was a rebellion.

There was also an implied insult in the fact that lambs were tied up in preparation for slaughter, for, as a Midrash (interpretation and explanation) on Exodus tells us, 'When the Holy One told Moses to slaughter the paschal lamb, Moses objected, "Do You not know that the lamb is an Egyptian god?" (compare Exodus 8:25–28). God replied, "On your life, Israel will not leave here until they slaughter the Egyptian gods before their very eyes, that I may teach them that their gods are really nothing at all."' (Exodus Rabbah 16:3)

Bearing in mind these ancient Jewish interpretations of the sabbath before Passover, we can see how upset the Egyptians would have been as the Israelites prepared to slaughter lambs, see the Egyptian firstborn die and then flee.

More significantly for Christians, this tradition tells us that the meal Jesus shared with Mary, Martha and Lazarus was very likely to have been the *Shabbat Hagadol*. The Passover was on the Thursday, the sabbath was five days before that, and Jesus visited Bethany on the sixth day before the Passover—that is, on the Friday. If we assume that the dinner Mary and Martha prepared was a meal to celebrate Jesus' visit and welcome him back, it was held on the Friday evening, the traditional time for a sabbath evening meal. (However, Mark 14:1 and Matthew 26:2 suggest that this meal took place on the Tuesday, two days before the Passover). But if Jesus returned to Bethany (the closest place to a home that he had), for a last meal on the last sabbath before the Passover, and that sabbath recalls the preparation of the lambs for the Passover, then here is a hint by John that Jesus is the new Passover Lamb of God, whose sacrifice will bring about a second exodus, delivering not only the Jews but all people.

At that meal in Bethany, whether it was six or two days before the Passover, Jesus and Lazarus enjoyed table fellowship. This must have been a great delight for them both, since it was not long previously that Lazarus had fallen ill, died and been raised (John 11). As they ate together, with Lazarus still alive and well, they would have talked, and we might suppose that the promise of resurrection could well have come up in conversation. Again, John is not explicit, but here is a meal that points us forward to the resurrection fellowship banquet of which the meals Jesus shares on earth are but foretastes.

Saviour Christ, who took time to be with your friends, to share table fellowship and celebrate the feasts of the Father, help us to speak of resurrection and hope, that people may desert the ways of the world and come to believe. Amen

HOLY WEEK

PALMS AND WHEAT

The next day the great crowd that had come to the festival heard that Jesus was coming to Jerusalem. So they took branches of palm trees and went out to meet him, shouting, 'Hosanna! Blessed is the one who comes in the name of the Lord—the King of Israel!' Jesus found a young donkey and sat on it; as it is written: 'Do not be afraid, daughter of Zion. Look, your king is coming, sitting on a donkey's colt!' His disciples did not understand these things at first... So the crowd that had been with him when he called Lazarus out of the tomb and raised him from the dead continued to testify. It was also because they heard that he had performed this sign that the crowd went to meet him...

Now among those who went up to worship at the festival were some Greeks. They came to Philip, who was from Bethsaida in Galilee, and said to him, 'Sir, we wish to see Jesus.' Philip went and told Andrew; then Andrew and Philip went and told Jesus. Jesus answered them, 'The hour has come for the Son of Man to be glorified. Very truly, I tell you, unless a grain of wheat falls into the earth and dies, it remains just a single grain; but if it dies, it bears much fruit.'

JOHN 12:12–24 (ABRIDGED)

We saw yesterday how Jesus returned to Bethany on the sabbath eve before the Passover festival. The next day, the sabbath (Saturday), Jesus entered Jerusalem and was hailed by the pilgrims who had travelled to Jerusalem to attend Passover. They left the city wanting to see Jesus, having heard that Lazarus had been raised. Their enthusiasm is Passover-inspired: their acclamations come directly from Psalm 118:26: 'Blessed is the one who comes in the name of the Lord. We bless you from the house of the Lord.' This psalm was a common processional one used as pilgrims went up to the 'house of the Lord' at Passover. As they approached, they would also sing, 'This is the gate of the Lord; the righteous shall enter through it' (v. 20) and 'Bind the festal procession with branches, up to the horns of the altar' (v. 27).

Thus it seems that these pilgrims, who were not residents of Jerusalem, had palm branches with them already when they came out to meet Jesus. By walking peaceably into Jerusalem, led by Jesus, they were to some extent doing what they might have done anyway. What is different, of course, is that in the context of the Passover procession into the temple, they hail Christ as king of Israel, waving palm fronds, which were symbols of victory. Their spontaneous enthusiasm served to aggravate Jesus' enemies further, hastening the final deadly showdown with the Jewish and Roman authorities.

Neither Jesus' old nor his new friends really understand what is going on. The disciples realize later, while his newfound fans, the Jewish pilgrims from the Greek diaspora (Jews living all over the Greek-speaking world), want to meet the celebrity Christ. The disciples act as Jesus' minders and there seems to have been some discussion between Andrew and Philip as to whether these foreigners should be allowed to meet him. We are not told that they actually got to do so. Instead, we hear Jesus' cryptic comment about wheat.

In first-century Palestine, wheat and barley were the two staple grain crops. Both are mentioned in Deuteronomy 8:8, where Israel is described as 'a land of wheat and barley, of vines and fig trees and pomegranates, a land of olive trees and honey'. Barley was harvested around Passover time (as described in Leviticus 23:5–10) and wheat around the time of Pentecost (see vv. 15–17). This means that, as the barley was harvested at Passover, it was a critical time for the growth of the wheat (see also Deuteronomy 16:1–9). Later, when the wheat was harvested, some of it would be offered in worship so that the summer fruit would do well. So when Jesus mentions wheat, he is referring to something that was very much in the minds of his hearers, who were hoping and praying that the wheat harvest would be good.

As they are thinking of the end of the wheat harvest, however, Jesus reminds them of the beginning of the cycle. Some grains of wheat must be kept as seeds for the following year. There can be no harvest unless there is first a death. The 'dead' seed is buried in the ground but after a time it sprouts, grows, emerges from the ground and bears fruit. In the same way, says Jesus, salvation is possible only by the death of the Son of God, who, though dead and buried, rises again, bringing new life as the fruit of resurrection. In the little grain of wheat analogy, Jesus explains everything that has gone before and that will follow. The palms the pilgrims are waving will represent the victory of the cross over death—the resurrection victory won by Christ, who, like a grain of wheat, died, was buried and rose again for our salvation.

Christ our king, as we proclaim the victory you have won over death, give us grace to die to self, that we too may bear much fruit to the furtherance of your kingdom on earth. Amen.

PASSOVER MARKET

The Passover of the Jews was near, and Jesus went up to Jerusalem. In the temple he found people selling cattle, sheep, and doves, and the money-changers seated at their tables. Making a whip of cords, he drove all of them out of the temple, both the sheep and the cattle. He also poured out the coins of the money-changers and overturned their tables. He told those who were selling the doves, 'Take these things out of here! Stop making my Father's house a marketplace! ... Destroy this temple, and in three days I will raise it up.' The Jews then said, 'This temple has been under construction for forty-six years, and will you raise it up in three days?' But he was speaking of the temple of his body.

JOHN 2:13–16, 19–21

A few weeks ago, we looked at the origins of the Passover in the events of the Israelites' escape from Egypt. The most important ingredient in Jesus' time was the Passover (or 'paschal') lamb, although nowadays it is not customary to eat lamb at Passover. This is because Passover can no longer be celebrated in the Jerusalem temple. (In AD70 the Romans destroyed it, as Jesus predicts in Matthew 24:1–2.)

For Jesus and his predecessors, the Passover would have been celebrated by eating paschal lamb that the temple priests had deemed to be pure and spotless. It was this authorization to which Jesus objected so much when he turned over the tables. Jewish families had a choice, to breed or purchase a lamb of their own or to buy one in the temple that had been pre-approved. Since there was a commercial interest for the temple authorities to sell the lambs they had acquired for the festival, it was not easy to gain their approval for 'external' lambs. Therefore most people bought their lambs in the temple, falling victim to what was effectively a monopoly.

The lambs would be purchased on the tenth day of the month of Nissan, to be sacrificed five days later (see 'Lazarus' sabbath supper', p. 130). On that day (the 15th of Nissan), silver trumpets were sounded by the priests as a signal to begin the slaughter. The fat was burned and the blood collected to be poured on to the base of the altar. No bone of the Passover lamb was to be broken (Numbers 9:12). Meanwhile, the assembled crowd sang a response to the Psalms: *Hallelu Yah* ('Praise the Lord').

It must have been quite an experience of sound, sight and smell. But after AD70 Jewish tables no longer had a Passover lamb with which to celebrate and, still to this day, orthodox Passover meals have only the shank bone of a lamb on their *seder* plate, indicating the absence of the Passover lamb. It is known as the *z'roah* ('arm'), and has its own symbolism, reminding partakers of God's outstretched arm to save his people (see Deuteronomy 26:8). Christ associated himself with the Passover lamb, and there is some irony in the fact that, as the Christian Church was beginning to take shape and increase, the Jewish Passover had to adapt to not having a lamb on the table. As Christians we might want to say that that was because, by the Holy Spirit, Christ the Passover sacrifice was alive and present in his Church and in the new paschal feast of the Eucharist—for it was the outstretched arm of Christ on the cross that ultimately saved God's people.

Other elements in the Passover also point us towards Christ: an egg (*betzah*) is also on the *seder* plate, and it symbolizes both mourning and the hope of spiritual restoration and resurrection.[24] While Jews mourn the loss of the temple, we may mourn Christ's passion while drawing hope from the new resurrection life that he gains for us by his sacrifice. Bitter herbs (*maror*) are used at the meal, which remind the eaters of the slavery in Egypt and inspire gratitude for deliverance. The herbs are dipped in salt water, representing both tears of hardship and the blood of the first paschal lambs. As Christians we may be reminded of the tears shed by Jesus for Jerusalem (Luke 19:41) and his own blood shed on the cross. Tears genuinely flow when grated horseradish (a second type of *maror*) is eaten. Parsley (*karpas*) signifies hyssop, with which the doorposts were painted (Exodus 12:22; also see 'John's Passover', p. 150). There would also have been *charoset* (a spiced fruit and nut mixture), which made the bitter herbs palatable. It might remind Christians of the spices used at the burial of Jesus (John 19:39–42). Finally, as well as the bread and wine there would have been salt, symbolizing the sacredness of the feast: 'with all your offerings you shall offer salt' (Leviticus 2:13). As Christians, we are reminded of Jesus' saying 'You are the salt of the earth' (Matthew 5:13), but in either case salt represents preservation, purity and steadfastness to God and neighbour.

God of the Passover, who sent Jesus Christ as your new lamb of deliverance, guard the integrity of our dealings and keep us true in business and in worship. Amen.

CHRIST OUR PASSOVER

Clean out the old yeast so that you may be a new batch, as you really are unleavened. For our paschal lamb, Christ, has been sacrificed. Therefore, let us celebrate the festival, not with the old yeast, the yeast of malice and evil, but with the unleavened bread of sincerity and truth...

The cup of blessing that we bless, is it not a sharing in the blood of Christ? The bread that we break, is it not a sharing in the body of Christ? Because there is one bread, we who are many are one body, for we all partake of the one bread...

The Lord Jesus on the night when he was betrayed took a loaf of bread, and when he had given thanks, he broke it and said, 'This is my body that is for you. Do this in remembrance of me.' In the same way he took the cup also, after supper, saying, 'This cup is the new covenant in my blood. Do this, as often as you drink it, in remembrance of me.' For as often as you eat this bread and drink the cup, you proclaim the Lord's death until he comes.

1 CORINTHIANS 5:7–8, 10:16–17, 11:23–26

As a formally zealous Jew (Galatians 1:14), Paul had no doubt about Christ's relationship to and fulfilment of major Passover hopes. The removal of leaven from the house was a key pre-Passover ritual. Leaven (yeast) makes bread rise, and Passover bread must be unleavened, like the bread the Israelites ate in Egypt before and after the tenth plague (Exodus 12:8–20, 39). Leaven represents sin, so the home is purged of sin before the meal can commence. This pre-Passover ritual, which is still practised in Judaism, is known as *Bedikat Chametz*, and there are similarities to be noticed with the Shrove Tuesday traditions that we find all over the world today (see p. 8), in which unwanted foods are purged from the house by consuming or destroying them. Thus sin, or the opportunity for sin, is removed. Paul refers to this kind of ritual in writing to the Corinthians, entreating them to adopt new ways and new beliefs about the hope and glory revealed in Jesus Christ, celebrated at the new paschal festival of Easter.

Then Paul mentions the 'cup of blessing': the third of four cups of wine drunk at the Passover. The first cup ('of sanctification') launches the meal; the second cup ('of praise') comes after questions and answers and teaching about the origins of Passover; the third cup ('of blessing' or 'redemption') is specifically reminiscent of the blood of the paschal lamb and follows thanksgivings for what has already been consumed. Finally, after all have sung Psalms 115—118 and a hymn (possibly entitled 'The breath of every living thing shall praise your name'), the final cup ('of acceptance') is blessed and shared. This cup, also sometimes known as 'the cup of Elijah', emphasizes the hope of messianic redemption: 'I will send you the prophet Elijah before the great and terrible day of the Lord comes' (Malachi 4:5).

At the time of Jesus, the Passover meal began with the dipping of bitter herbs into salty water or vinegar (see 'Passover market, p. 138). Then, after the second cup of wine had been drunk, there would have been a ceremonial hand-washing before touching the unleavened bread, which the host broke after having said a prayer of blessing. This kind of prayer is called a *berakah* and it survives even amid today's eucharistic celebrations. The first of these blessings would be said over the first cup of wine and was known as the *Kiddush*: 'Blessed art thou, O Lord our God, who hast created the fruit of the vine…'.[25] The breaking of bread was accompanied by two prayers, one giving thanks for the bread itself and the other giving thanks for the commandment to eat unleavened bread at this time. The fact that it was broken and shared among everyone reminded them that the poor had only broken bread to eat.

This was *not* the bread of which Jesus said, 'This is my body', for later in the meal, 'after supper', he took another piece of bread and added a second breaking of bread. The first, prescribed breaking of bread, dipped in bitter herbs and *charoseth* (see p. 139), is what was distributed before Judas left the meal (see p. 144), and was preceded by the first ceremonial washing, whereby Jesus went so far as to wash not merely his own hands but their feet (see John 13:3–11). Jesus' taking of the bread came effectively after the meal was ended, at the point at which it was traditional to say thanksgiving prayers, rather like a 'grace' after a meal. Jesus enhanced that tradition and pointed it towards himself by adding a second bread breaking, declaring that it was his body, broken for them. While Jesus' taking of the cup, as Paul calls it, was already part of the Passover meal (it would have been the third cup), the breaking of bread was new. After he had done this, they all sang the traditional final hymn and left (see Matthew 26:30).

In celebrating a Passover meal with his disciples, Jesus combined the old and the new. He reinvented the Passover by declaring himself the Passover lamb, long-awaited and promised. His actions were clear to those present, and Paul understood perfectly, explaining them to the Corinthians. Thus, in creating a remembrance of the new covenant in the midst of a celebration of the old, Jesus redefined Passover and offered himself as an a explanation of its hopes and meaning.

Christ our Passover, you have been sacrificed for us, yet you share the bread of yourself with sinners. Respond to our poor thanksgivings and offerings of praise with your customary loving kindness, now and always. Amen

JUDAS' SOP

[Jesus said] '"The one who ate my bread has lifted his heel against me." I tell you this now, before it occurs, so that when it does occur, you may believe that I am he. Very truly, I tell you, whoever receives one whom I send receives me; and whoever receives me receives him who sent me.' After saying this Jesus was troubled in spirit, and declared, 'Very truly, I tell you, one of you will betray me.' The disciples looked at one another, uncertain of whom he was speaking. One of his disciples—the one whom Jesus loved—was reclining next to him; Simon Peter therefore motioned to him to ask Jesus of whom he was speaking. So while reclining next to Jesus, he asked him, 'Lord, who is it?' Jesus answered, 'It is the one to whom I give this piece of bread when I have dipped it in the dish.' So when he had dipped the piece of bread, he gave it to Judas son of Simon Iscariot. After he received the piece of bread, Satan entered into him. Jesus said to him, 'Do quickly what you are going to do.' Now no one at the table knew why he said this to him. Some thought that, because Judas had the common purse, Jesus was telling him, 'Buy what we need for the festival'; or, that he should give something to the poor. So, after receiving the piece of bread, he immediately went out.

JOHN 13:18–30

The meal we have come to call 'the last supper' was effectively Jesus' final symposium (see 'Christ's symposium', p. 124). It is easy to form a vague impression of the last supper as the occasion when Jesus shared the Passover with his disciples, during which he washed their feet, had a row with Judas, predicted Peter's denials, invented Holy Communion and gave a 'farewell discourse'.

Judas had reclined at many meals with Jesus but he does not stay long at this final one. He would have attended many Passover meals as a boy, perhaps sometimes as the youngest present, when he would have asked his father the question, 'Why is this night different from all other nights, and why do we eat unleavened bread?' Thus the storytelling part of the ancient *seder* meal would commence, in which is recounted the origin and history of the feast, beginning with the call of Abraham and moving through to the deliverance from Egypt and the giving of the Ten Commandments. The head of the household would also relate how the fleeing Israelites had time only to prepare unleavened bread.

The youngest son would then ask about the eating of bitter herbs and would be told that they represent the bitterness of hardship under Pharaoh in Egypt. Then he would ask about why the lamb is roasted, not stewed or boiled. To this question he would be told how the roasting of the meat symbolized judgment. Next, Psalms 113 and 114 would be sung and a second cup of wine drunk. As we saw yesterday, the bread would then be broken by the host, who prayed blessings and thanksgivings, and a piece given to each person to dip into the bitter herbs and *charoseth*.

This broken bread was called the 'sop', and to be offered this 'sop' first was a special favour—a sign of honour and love. It's also worth remembering that at this juncture, Jesus had already washed the disciples' feet (John 13:4–12), including those of Judas. Jesus knew, as he knelt before Judas, that this dirty-footed man was going to hand him over, yet he continued to show him love and respect at the Passover table, and it is likely that he offered Judas the 'sop' first.

Judas had already planned his betrayal and been paid by Caiaphas and the high priests (Matthew 26:14–16). Jesus may have known this or may have sensed it in Judas' behaviour. Judas realizes he is discovered and leaves. Days later, he would feel remorse, repent and hang himself (27:3–10). But the penultimate encounter between Jesus and Judas, before the fateful kiss of peace in the garden of Gethsemane by which Judas betrayed Jesus (26:48–49), is when Jesus gives him bread—the substance of life, doled out as Jesus himself becomes the bread of life, broken for a broken world. Jesus gives his bread, himself, not only to his friends but also to those broken by sin. We have seen him dining with tax collectors and sinners and being criticized for it. Now, at the last supper he dines with those who are both friends and sinners. His friends, Judas among them, are sinners and they let him down. Yet Jesus still shares his bread and offers himself so that their sin may be replaced with the friendship of God himself.

Lord, you share your bread with sinners yet count us as your friends. We thank you, we bless you, we praise you. Amen

CHRIST'S COMMUNION FEAST

When the hour came, [Jesus] took his place at the table, and the apostles with him. He said to them, 'I have eagerly desired to eat this Passover with you before I suffer; for I tell you, I will not eat it until it is fulfilled in the kingdom of God.' Then he took a cup, and after giving thanks he said, 'Take this and divide it among yourselves; for I tell you that from now on I will not drink of the fruit of the vine until the kingdom of God comes.' Then he took a loaf of bread, and when he had given thanks, he broke it and gave it to them, saying, 'This is my body, which is given for you. Do this in remembrance of me.' And he did the same with the cup after supper, saying, 'This cup that is poured out for you is the new covenant in my blood.'

LUKE 22:14–20

In the UK, approximately three quarters of a billion bottles of wine are consumed annually: that's 14 litres per person, or one glass a week. With bread, these figures are dwarfed: nine million loaves are consumed in the UK each day, an average of three and a half slices each. Do you have toast for breakfast or sandwiches for lunch? Most people do, it seems. Bread is, in fact, our daily bread, our staple diet.

While bread and wine do not have quite the same significance for us as they did for first-century Jews, they are still very important in today's diet. Both have an ancient history: as we have seen, Noah is considered the first wine maker (Genesis 9:20), and references to bread take us back to God's curse on Adam, when God says, 'By the sweat of your face you shall eat bread until you return to the ground,

146

for out of it you were taken; you are dust, and to dust you shall return' (Genesis 3:19). This text is more often remembered for the words with which we begin Lent, when the sign of the cross is made in ash on the forehead and the priest says, 'From dust you were made and to dust you shall return.'

We have always needed and enjoyed bread and wine. They feature significantly in the Passover meal commemorating the exodus from Egypt, and Jesus wished to share that feast with his disciples before the final agony and triumphant victory of cross and resurrection. Jesus does not simply recall history or merely eat a meal, but he reinterprets the Jewish Passover meal in respect of himself as Saviour and Son of God. In the *seder*, the host recounts the story of the exodus, describing how God liberated his people, and here in the new Passover the old covenant between God and Abraham is realigned to reflect a new covenant, enacted in broken bread and wine shared. These ingredients are not new: they were always integral to the Passover ritual.

In 'On Pascha', the earliest Christian sermon that has survived from antiquity (written around AD167 or 168), Bishop Melito of Sardis spells out the connection between Jesus and the Passover tradition that Jesus described himself as fulfilling:

He is the Pascha of our salvation. It is he who in many endured many things: It is he that was in Abel murdered, and in Isaac bound, and in Jacob exiled, and in Joseph sold, and in Moses exposed, and in the lamb slain, and in David persecuted, and in the prophets dishonoured. It is he that was enfleshed in a virgin, that was hanged on a tree. It is he that has been murdered.[26]

Eighteen hundred years after Melito, who was himself writing only 150 years after Christ, we can still reflect on how Jesus takes Passover bread and wine and gives the ritual a new, self-referential meaning. We still celebrate Communion in this manner. Some church communities even re-enact the Passover meal on this day. But at every Communion service we recall that event by celebrating a part of it, daily, weekly or quarterly. Especially on Maundy Thursday, we remember and give thanks for the gift of Christ to his people—the gift and the command to 'do this in remembrance of me'. In some churches today, the liturgy is changed to 'on *this* night that he was betrayed', adding poignancy and power to the celebration and remembrance of Jesus' institution of the Eucharist.

It is in bread and wine that Christ's earthly presence is recalled—earthly and earthy, for both are products of ancient and sophisticated crafts that utilize God's bounty for physical survival. Yet as we have already seen, Christ is spiritually present in bread and wine too, and we need him for spiritual survival (see 'Eucharistic food', p. 113). Today we celebrate and give thanks for it especially. We lament what followed but rejoice in the Easter dawn that is surely to come, in the light of which we bathe, even in the darkest hours of Good Friday.

Lord Christ, you honour us in offering us the bread of your body and the wine of your blood. As we are fed and nourished in body and soul, may our hearts and minds be always lifted to you, from whom come all good gifts and salvation itself. Amen.

JOHN'S PASSOVER

They took Jesus from Caiaphas to Pilate's headquarters. It was early in the morning. They themselves did not enter the headquarters, so as to avoid ritual defilement and to be able to eat the Passover... [Pilate] told them, 'I find no case against him. But you have a custom that I release someone for you at the Passover. Do you want me to release for you the King of the Jews?' They shouted in reply, 'Not this man, but Barabbas!' Now Barabbas was a bandit...

After this, when Jesus knew that all was now finished, he said (in order to fulfil the scripture), 'I am thirsty.' A jar full of sour wine was standing there. So they put a sponge full of the wine on a branch of hyssop and held it to his mouth. When Jesus had received the wine, he said, 'It is finished.' Then he bowed his head and gave up his spirit. Since it was the day of Preparation, the Jews did not want the bodies left on the cross during the sabbath, especially because that sabbath was a day of great solemnity. So they asked Pilate to have the legs of the crucified men broken and the bodies removed. Then the soldiers came and broke the legs of the first and of the other who had been crucified with him. But when they came to Jesus and saw that he was already dead, they did not break his legs. Instead, one of the soldiers pierced his side with a spear, and at once blood and water came out.

JOHN 18:28, 38–40; 19:28–34

There is a trend in popular piety to see Pilate as a kind of victim: a man with a dreaming wife who is overruled by the crowd, who tries to save Christ by negotiating first with King Herod and then by offering to release Jesus. Yet Pilate was the governor of Judea: he was in charge of Jerusalem and his word was decisive and final. He wanted Jesus out of the way as much as anyone else did: Jesus was dangerous politically as well as annoying in religious terms. Since they held power in the land, only the Romans could lay on something as extravagantly horrible as crucifixion. By way of strange homage to their imperial landlords, the Jewish leaders wanted the full works for the wining and dining teacher and preacher whom they hated so much, but who had been hailed as king less than a week earlier. Pilate gave Christ his cross, and Christ bled and died upon it.

While Matthew, Mark and Luke present the last supper as a Passover meal, in the context of which Jesus relocates the story of salvation in himself, John indicates that they celebrated a day earlier. He makes no specific mention of a Passover meal and, with powerful symbolism, describes Christ dying on the cross at the same time as the lambs for the Passover are being slaughtered.

While on the cross, Jesus accepts a sponge, skewered on a branch of hyssop, that has been dipped in wine. The hyssop that the soldiers use is significant, for the plant was used as a kind of paintbrush to brush the doors and lintels before the original Passover (Exodus 12:22). Hyssop was probably more like what we know as marjoram, and represents lowliness (1 Kings 4:33) and cleansing ('Purge me with hyssop', Psalm 51:7). This emphasizes the sacrifice that Jesus, the Lamb of God, has made in shedding his blood. Hyssop also had medicinal uses, mostly associated with the prevention or reduction of infection (particularly leprosy)—according to Leviticus 14:49–51, a branch of hyssop was used to cleanse the house after such infection had been eradicated—but it seems unlikely that the Roman soldiers had this in mind.

For John, Christ truly is 'the Lamb of God who takes away the sin of the world!' (John 1:29, 36). We can say with some confidence that the last supper was a kind of Passover meal, and therefore the death of Christ at this time adds action to the words he says when breaking the bread. A Passover crucifixion underlines the connections between Jesus and the sacrificial lamb of Exodus 12 (see p. 46), and thus invites the inevitable conclusion that Jesus' death on the cross must be seen in the context of the bigger picture of God's redemption of Israel. His death is the culmination of that story, and, after the resurrection, becomes the first part of a story in which God redeems not only Israel but all who come to believe that Jesus is the sacrificial Lamb of God who pays the deadly price of universal sin and defeats death by rising on the third day. John writes of blood and water flowing from Christ's pierced side: this not only proves that he was dead, but this brutal act, reminiscent of slaughter, releases the blood of redemption and the living water of new spiritual life.

Jesus, Lamb of God, you take away the sins of the world. Have mercy on us and grant us peace. As your holy blood cleanses us, accept us into the joy of the eternal banquet of the kingdom, where you reign, crucified in glory, raised from pain and death, now and for ever. Amen

EMMAUS SUPPER

Two of them were going to a village called Emmaus, about seven miles from Jerusalem… While they were talking and discussing, Jesus himself came near and went with them, but their eyes were kept from recognizing him… As they came near the village to which they were going, he walked ahead as if he were going on. But they urged him strongly, saying, 'Stay with us, because it is almost evening and the day is now nearly over.' So he went in to stay with them. When he was at the table with them, he took bread, blessed and broke it, and gave it to them. Then their eyes were opened, and they recognized him; and he vanished from their sight. They said to each other, 'Were not our hearts burning within us while he was talking to us on the road, while he was opening the scriptures to us?'
LUKE 24:13–16, 28–32

Today is a day on which we look back and forward. Yesterday we 'celebrated' Good Friday, the day on which our Lord suffered excruciating pain and humiliation but, in dying like a paschal lamb, opened up our way to salvation. Tomorrow—or tonight in places that celebrate a Vigil or Easter Eve service—we welcome the risen Christ with alleluias and rejoicing. The journey to Easter is reaching its conclusion. Yet for the fledgling Christian Church it was barely beginning, and this story of the disciples on the road to Emmaus illustrates how far they had to go. Jesus has to explain the scriptures as they relate to himself, and it is only when they sit down and eat together that he reveals himself to them in the blessing and breaking of bread. Until this moment, 'they were kept from recognizing him'. But then they invite Christ to dine with them—a simple but obvious act of fellowship and hospitality to a stranger who has become a friend and teacher on the way. This reminds us that it is not our action, will or ability that gives us wisdom or even faith, but it is the gift and action of Christ himself that inspires and enables the hospitality of our hearts. It is in giving that we ultimately receive.

I am reminded of that lovely Danish story of Babette's feast, written by Isak Dinesen (real name Karen Blixen, of *Out of Africa* fame). The story was published in 1958, and Gabriel Axel's film adaptation won an Oscar in 1986. Babette, a French refugee, becomes the cook to a puritanical household in Jutland. Their diet is simple, even boring, but she begins to liven it up, causing a mixture of delight and approbation. In due course, she wins the lottery and, with their begrudging permission, persuades the community to let her prepare a sumptuous feast. Unbeknown to them, she spends the whole of her winnings on food and wine imported from France, which she prepares with love and skill. Guests are invited and, as the evening progresses, wonderful dishes emerge from the kitchen and cold hearts are surprised by the joy of good food, wine and company. When the guests have departed and the washing-up is done, it is clear that something indescribably amazing has happened—an almost divine transformation. Scales have fallen from hearts, reconciliation has occurred and a new future beckons.

Many have seen in this film overtones of eucharistic transformation, by which Babette's diners become a new body of Christ, transubstantiated by the love and sacrifice that she has expended without regard to cost or effort. The meal she prepares is a selfless act; she cannot enjoy the meal itself but takes a greater, providential pleasure in the delight she brings to others through her cooking.

All cooks know something of the joyful challenge that preparing food for others brings. A blend of art and science, cookery is an act of love and effort that meets both needs and desires, fuelling fellowship and promoting well-being. To be able to cook well is indeed a privilege. But not everybody needs to be a cook; indeed, the disciples on the road to Emmaus were probably not, and invited Jesus to share a meal that was no doubt provided by some other unseen host, whom they paid. (I wonder who had the unknown honour of providing that supper on the road to Emmaus!)

In this story, both guest and host are in a sense unseen. A popular inscription often found in the home describes Christ as 'the unseen guest at every meal', but he is also the host of every meal, be it Eucharist or frugal supper. On this day when Christ disappears from our liturgies, buried in the tomb, to rise tomorrow, we do well to remember that at our invitation he reveals himself in scripture and sacrament, and in return invites us to dine with him at the most lavish banquet ever offered in heaven or earth.

Christ, the unseen guest at our table, bless all the food you provide for our use, and us in the service of your kingdom, so that we may meet you in those whom we meet on our road, and always thank you for your goodness. Amen

PETER'S BREAKFAST

Simon Peter said to them, 'I am going fishing.' They said to him, 'We will go with you.' They went out and got into the boat, but that night they caught nothing. Just after daybreak, Jesus stood on the beach; but the disciples did not know that it was Jesus. Jesus said to them, 'Children, you have no fish, have you?' They answered him, 'No.' He said to them, 'Cast the net to the right side of the boat, and you will find some.' So they cast it, and now they were not able to haul it in because there were so many fish... When they had gone ashore, they saw a charcoal fire there, with fish on it, and bread. Jesus said to them, 'Bring some of the fish that you have just caught.' So Simon Peter went aboard and hauled the net ashore, full of large fish, a hundred and fifty-three of them; and though there were so many, the net was not torn. Jesus said to them, 'Come and have breakfast.' Now none of the disciples dared to ask him, 'Who are you?' because they knew it was the Lord. Jesus came and took the bread and gave it to them, and did the same with the fish.

JOHN 21:3–6, 9–13

The 18th-century French philosopher Jean-Anthelme Brillat-Savarin (1755–1828) wrote a treatise called *La Physiologie de goût*, known in English as *The Philosopher in the Kitchen*. It is a delightful, quirky book, with recipes, musings on food and drink and the occasional digression into theology and philosophy.

Sandwiched between a chapter on drinks and another on gourmandism (the enjoyment of good food) is a brief observation about the likelihood of our planet being struck by a comet, a possibility of which Brillat-Savarin was well aware. In 1793 he was elected Mayor of his home town, Belley, but the French Revolution forced him to flee to Switzerland and then America, where he taught French and played in the orchestra of the New York Theatre. But his gastronomical musings were not simply about food: he was concerned with the wider and deeper issues associated with eating. Discussing what he called the 'pleasures of the table', he claimed that a good dinner is not just about the well-cooked fish, meat and vegetables; it is also an experience of good company, good conversation, visual delight, friendship and fellowship. He wrote:

The pleasure of eating is common to ourselves and the animals, and depends on nothing but hunger and the means to satisfy it. The pleasures of the table are peculiar to mankind, and depend on preliminary care over the preparation of the meal, the choice of the place, and the selection of the guests... When the need for food begins to be satisfied, then the intellect awakes, talk becomes general, a new order of things is initiated, and he who until then was a mere consumer of food becomes a table companion of more or less charm, according to the qualities of nature bestowed upon him by the Master of all things.[27]

Brillat-Savarin introduces a spiritual dimension to eating meals and reminds us that dining together can have transforming power. It is in the spirit of Christian fellowship that many churches nowadays share what we might call an *agape* meal. The post-resurrection meeting of Peter and Christ truly is an *agape* meal—a meal in which the satisfying of hunger gives way to deeper, loving, transforming fellowship, in which forgiveness, restoration and commission take place.

We are reminded of another courtyard and another charcoal fire, around which Peter denied Christ three times (John 18:15–27). It is often said of this passage that Jesus asks Peter three times if he loves him, each time erasing a denial. In Greek there are three words for love, and in this story it matters. *Eros* is sexual, *philia* is linked to friendship, and *agape* usually refers to a sacrificial, total commitment. Jesus asks Peter twice if he loves him using the verb *agape*. Each time, Peter replies using the word *philia*. The third time, Jesus uses *philia* himself and Peter gets upset. He affirms his *philia* once again—indeed, it is what he has been saying all along. Yet Peter has been evading Jesus' questions, suggesting that he cannot love Christ as Christ loves him, in a self-sacrificing, committed way (*agape*).

Nevertheless, Peter is released from the bonds of his denial and his rock-like status is restored to him as Jesus accepts what love he can offer and works with it, commissioning Peter to go and pastor his flock. It is a terrifying, humbling and fantastic moment, in which, over a meal, 'a new order of things is initiated', as Brillat-Savarin put it.

This story of a resurrection breakfast shows us that Christ, our risen paschal lamb, is with us whenever we share table fellowship in a spirit of either *agape* or *philia*. And that is a pleasure of the table that may be enjoyed both on earth and in heaven.

As we celebrate your resurrection, Lord, grace us with your presence when we dine, for all tables are yours and all companionship transformed when enjoyed under the banner of your love. Amen

⁜

LENT ACTIVITIES AND GROUP MATERIAL

It is always good to meet together in groups for learning and fellowship. These questions and exercises are offered in order to facilitate leaders and group members alike, and should not be seen as restrictive or conclusive. Local custom and desire will determine whether eating together before or after a group meeting is appropriate, possible or desirable.

Group leaders are strongly advised to read through these notes before the course begins, so that additional resources may be acquired if necessary. Internet research or a copy of Rex Russell's book *What The Bible Says About Healthy Living* (Regal Books, 1999) will certainly stimulate discussion if someone has familiarized themselves with food health issues, which can barely be touched upon in this book.

Introduction: Food and sin

- What did you do on Shrove Tuesday? Was the day marked in any way: did you 'eat up' eggs and flour or make pancakes or other seasonal foods? Share any experiences you have of Shrove Tuesdays at various times and places.

- What did you do on Ash Wednesday? Did you go to church or not? Why (not)? What is Lent about, for you? Is it relevant today to associate it with food or is that an old-fashioned, irrelevant dimension now?

- What does it mean to be tempted? Spend a few minutes alone or in pairs contemplating when you were last tempted and how you responded. Are you the kind of person who is easily tempted? Are you the kind of person who readily succumbs? (These are two different questions!)

- Do you think that food or drink comes between you and God? How might it for you or others, and what can be done?

- Remembering the story of Cain and Abel (you might like to read it together), consider how, even today, food issues cause the deaths of our brothers and sisters. Reflect together on how much sin is involved in eating and food production. It might be useful for someone to make notes on what you say or conclude, for later reference.

Week One: Humans and other animals

- Think about and recall what is in your fridge. Do the labels on the animal products you buy tell you anything about the way in which those animals were cared for? Do you understand the labels? Could they be improved? (It may help if the host or another person has some packages handy for reference.)

- Do you know of any companies or products that are involved in animal testing, or refuse to get involved? Share your information. Do you agree with the Banner Committee's views on animal testing? Could the recommendations be improved or should they be altered? What do you think about giving mice cancer for the furtherance of cancer research? Would you rather the mouse had cancer than you?

- Think about genetic engineering and the manipulation of animals and foods. What do you know about these processes? Do some research either before or during the group meeting. Have a look at Psalm 100: what does it suggest about the way in which we are made and how we might react to human attempts to control creation?

- How many people in the group have or have had pets? How were they acquired? How did they die? Share some of your stories.

- Do animals have rights? Or is it more useful to consider our responsibilities towards them? As Christians, what do you think we should be doing about animal welfare, farming and testing? How important is this issue?

Week Two: Jacob, Joseph and the Jewish Passover

- What do you think about the story of Jacob and Esau? Was Jacob's behaviour acceptable? Remind yourselves of the story of his life: was he one of God's good guys? What happened in the end?

- How important is food in Joseph's story? Share among yourselves what you know about Egyptian history and culture and try to reconcile the story of Joseph with what you may know or discover about pyramids, Pharaohs and mummies.

- In what sense can the food that we eat today be compared with manna from heaven? The Israelites hardly worked for their food in the wilderness, yet when they tried to store it, it went bad. In what sense do we work for our food? Do you hoard food, and if so, why? Do the economics and practicalities of our supermarket culture distance us from the source of our food, and what can we do to remind ourselves that all gifts come from God?

- Have you ever had to prepare and eat a meal in haste, and if so, why? If someone told you to do something like this today, would you? Why do you think the Israelites did what they were told?

- You might find it useful to share what you know about the celebration of the Passover, its origins, original practice and modern-day celebration. The books *Christ in the Passover: Why is this Night Different?* (Ceil and Moishe Rosen, Moody Press, 1978) and *Passover Haggadah: A Messianic Celebration* (Eric-Peter Lipson, Purple Pomegranate, 2nd edition, 1988) will help, or the following websites may be helpful.

  ✣ www.bbc.co.uk/food/news_and_events/events_passovermeal.shtml
  ✣ http://en.wikipedia.org/wiki/Passover_Seder
  ✣ www.domini.org/tabern/passover.htm
  ✣ www.westarkchurchofchrist.org/wings/lbcexo11-12.htm

- You may even want to demonstrate or prepare a Passover table for the meeting (see 'What to eat', p. 167). If you can get hold of some of the ingredients (or substitutes for them), talk through what happens at a typical Passover. Try to get inside the Jewish perspective but also contemplate how any of it relates to Jesus.

Week Three: Food orders and disorders

If you are not a vegetarian, try avoiding meat (or all animal products) for a week, or for one day a week from now on during Lent. How does it make you feel? Do you think there is any point in doing so? How can we eat healthily with or without meat? Share your feelings about and experiences of vegetarianism in the group (remember to be sensitive to those with strong views and avoid being judgmental). The book *What The Bible Says About Healthy Living* may be very helpful for this week's session if someone can get a copy.

- Discuss in pairs or larger groups what connections between health and food you know about. How might dieting or fasting affect health? Share success stories if appropriate.

- What do you think about prohibition and permission relating to what we can, cannot, should or should not eat? Imagine yourself as a post-exodus Israelite: Why did God hand down prohibitions? Are such prohibitions necessary or desirable today? (Try to avoid lengthy anecdotal discussion about observant or non-observant Jewish people—that's not the point.) When it comes to food laws, does being a Christian make any difference? Read Acts 10:9–28: does this mean we can eat anything or is this passage more about the 'opening up' of the Gospel to both Gentiles and Jews?

- Do you know why it could ever be dangerous to eat shellfish and pork? As a group, attempt to devise some food laws for Christians today.

- Can people be blamed for their food dependencies? Share your thoughts and experiences of fasting, anorexia, gluttony and obesity. Are these personal or community issues? Be honest, but also be sensitive to others' experiences which you may not know about.

Week Four: Families, feasting and forgetting

- What is a feast? Share stories of 'feasts' you may have attended. What was good about them and what was bad? How do 'feasts' and feast days interconnect? Name as many feast days of the Church that you can. Are some feast days more important than others? Why?

- There is a great tradition in Orthodox Christian countries of an Easter feast with roast lamb. Celebrations involve cracking dyed red eggs, and the various foods that are found on the resurrection table have significance: *hiroméri* (smoked salted pork), cheeses, *magirítsa* (a creamy, lemony soup made from the lamb sweetmeats), *kouloúra* (Greek Easter bread), *tsoureki*, *lambropsomo* and other

Easter breads and plenty of wine, *retsina* and *ouzo*. The lamb (or goat) is served in honour of the Lamb of God. Have you ever celebrated such a feast? Would you like to?

- How often do you eat together in your families? Is that a positive experience or not? Is it true that families who 'eat together stay together'? What are the stresses of family dining, and what is to be gained? What are the advantages and disadvantages of eating alone?

- Do you say 'grace' before meals at home? If not, why not? Have we simply forgotten how to? What possible justification is there for not doing so? Think about situations in which 'grace' is not said and of the opportunities for mission and evangelism that doing so might provide. In what sense do we provide our food and in what sense does God?

- What is the most you have paid for a meal? (You might like to discuss this in pairs or small groups.) Why did you pay this much? Did you have a choice? How often do you eat out, or do you prefer to cook (or be cooked for) at home, and why?

- What do you think about large banquets where quantities of food are consumed at great expense? Are they unacceptable? Why (not)? How do today's banquets relate to the idea of a heavenly banquet prepared for the redeemed? What would Jesus say, do or think about modern feasting?

Week Five: A passion for Eucharist

- Watch the film *Babette's Feast* (see p. 153). If you are unable to do so, these questions may still yield an interesting discussion.

If you have watched the film:

- Share your immediate reactions. What is going on under the surface of the story? What can we learn about self-denial and enjoyment? Which characters in the film do you relate to best? What does Babette feel for her employers? What do they feel for her? Do they deserve what she does for them? Was it a good use of resources? Why does she do it? Would you want/be able to do that?

Other questions (if there is time, or for those who do not watch the film):

- Have a discussion about cooking. Who are the good cooks? Who dislikes cooking? How do people learn to cook? Is cooking about serving a need by providing food, or is it a bit more than that? Share your experiences of cooking and providing. What is the relationship between cookery and love?

- Where does fast food fit into all this? What does the popularity and ready availability of hamburgers say about society? Why do people turn to fast food, and is this a good thing?

If you have not managed to watch the film and still have time left, perhaps go back and look at questions in previous weeks that you did not have time for.

Week Six: Holy Week

You might like to celebrate an *agape* meal: a supper during which a Eucharist can be celebrated. This kind of meal can take place in a church hall or in someone's home, but most denominations insist that a suitably ordained minister celebrate at least the eucharistic part of the service. A ceremonial washing of the feet could also be included, before or after the Gospel reading. There is a lot of potential (and a lot of benefit) in such a meal; here I have only indicated how it *might* be done. Local custom and desire will determine a great deal.

For Anglicans, Roman Catholics or Methodists it could take this form:

- Hymn(s) or chorus(es)
- Greeting—Collect for Purity—*Kyries* ('Lord have mercy')—Confession and absolution
- Prayer or Collect (the provision for Maundy Thursday may be used for this kind of occasion)
- *Gloria* or hymn or song

- STARTER (optional) (such as soup and bread)
- Old and/or New Testament readings—hymn or song—Gospel reading—Sermon or meditation if desired)
- MAIN COURSE (such as baked potatoes/pasta/salad)
- Intercessions
- DESSERT (such as fruit or cake)
- Eucharistic Prayer (for example, *Common Worship* Prayer H or other more informal alternative), with sung *Sanctus* or other hymn or song praising God.
- Lord's Prayer—Prayer of Humble Access
- Distribution of Communion around the table(s)
- Post-Communion prayer—hymn or song—Blessing or grace

An alternative might be to include the elements of a Passover meal, but an *agape* meal is simpler to organize and conduct.

Week Seven: Beyond Easter (optional)

I have found in parish life that it is very difficult to fit in a Lent course session during Holy Week itself, because of services and other events that rightly take up time. This can mean, however, that the Lent course is never properly concluded. Therefore, if appropriate and desired, here are some questions and pointers for a final session that could take place after Easter, when the whole book has been read and when a meeting takes place in the context of resurrection hope and joy.

- What are the pleasures of the table? What can the pleasures of the table teach us about Holy Communion?

- Is there any sense in which we can speak of a 'calling' when it comes to the celebration of Holy Communion? What does our participation in bread and wine imply for the way in which we eat and drink in the world? Is there any sense in which we can speak of a vocation when we consider our attitudes towards the food we eat, either in terms of being called to cook for and serve others, or in terms of how we do our shopping and preparation of food?

- In the first week, we reflected on how food and sin are related. Try to recall what you said then (easy if someone took notes!) and consider whether your opinions have changed. To what extent are we the perpetrators of pain and grief on others through our consumption of food, and what can we do about it?

- To what extent are we the bringers of pain and grief to ourselves through our consumption, and what can we do about it?

- Did anyone choose to fast in any respect during Lent? How did you do? Has it made a difference? Will it have made a difference in six months' time?

- Concerning food, has anything changed for you in these last few weeks?

- Has this book made any difference? (Be honest; I won't be there!)

❖

WHAT TO EAT

If you are meeting in groups and want to include meal fellowship together, here are some suggested foods that might be easily prepared by a member of the group. Bear in mind that eating food together, rather than simply serving tea or coffee, will necessitate having a longer slot for the meeting, perhaps two hours.

Introduction

I know Lent has already started, but there is no biblical prohibition against pancakes! You can eat them if you talk about them too. You might also try some of the seasonal food that is consumed in other parts of the world (see p. 8).

Week One

Try Jacob's stew (see p. 36 for the recipe). If, like me, you don't like lentils much, consider it as a Lenten discipline to eat them anyway. If it helps, add bacon (not very authentic, I'm afraid…). Alternatively, buy ready-made lentil soup. Covent Garden soups and various supermarkets should be able to oblige if you are happy to use them.

Week Two

Try to gather as many of the ingredients for a Passover meal that you can find. Bitter herbs (parsley), horseradish, eggs, apples and raisins, salt water, red wine and pitta bread or matzos are a good start. This may not make a very satisfying meal in itself, so perhaps follow a 'tasting' of these ingredients with pasties (easy to serve), or even with traditional Jewish dishes, such as chicken soup with matzo balls.

Week Three

Have a bring-and-share lunch or supper when you meet this week. It may help to work out who will bring what, or you can take a chance and leave it completely open.

Week Four

A fish meal might be good this week, as we have now looked at a couple of passages about fish. A very simple option would be tuna pasta (preparation time 10 minutes).

Use tinned tuna: for each five people present, you need two small tins of tuna fish in oil (preferably olive oil if you can find it, but *not* brine, and make sure it is 'dolphin-friendly'), one carton of chopped tomatoes (*passata*), some Italian herbs (basil, oregano or similar) and a splash of red wine and some black pepper. Chopped green peppers and/or sliced olives may also be added. 100g of pasta per person should be enough, but you can be more generous. It is best not to use spaghetti for this dish; penne, fusili or other 'short' pasta would be preferable.

Pasta should be boiled on the hob according to the instructions on the packet. For best results, however, cook dried pasta for one minute less than it says on the packet. Dried pasta may take ten minutes, fresh only two minutes, but in either case do not be tempted to cook it longer than the instructions say. Some people add salt or olive oil to the water, but neither is necessary.

While the water is boiling and the pasta cooks, put all the other ingredients into a dish and either microwave the whole lot together until piping hot (times will vary in a microwave according to the quantity being made), or simmer. Since none of the ingredients actually needs to be cooked, there is no risk of undercooking here— just make sure it gets hot.

When the pasta is cooked, drain it thoroughly and decant it into a large bowl. Pour the hot tuna sauce on top, and mix thoroughly before serving. A rustic Italian red wine will go well, but do not add cheese to this dish. *Buon appetito!*

If vegetarian food is preferred, follow this recipe with aubergines (egg plant) instead of tuna, and add olive oil at the beginning. Grated Parmesan cheese is allowed with this version.

Week Five

By now, you may have discovered someone in the group who is a good cook and who would like to share their speciality. Ask them if they would be willing to prepare something for everyone, and express your appreciation for them. Then have a feast. How about rounding off your gathering by watching the film?

Otherwise, get a takeaway and share the cost. Pizzas go a long way when bought for a large group.

Holy Week

See page 164 for simple meal suggestions for an *agape* meal. You might want to make the meal available to those who are not necessarily part of a Lent group, as it can be a lovely form of fellowship for Holy Week anyway.

Final session

Do what you like! Book a restaurant, get a takeaway, have breakfast on a beach. Celebrate: the Lord is risen, Alleluia!

❖

PRAYER AND WORSHIP

Lent groups are an opportunity to share stories and insights in a safe, friendly and prayerful environment. Do not neglect to pray before and after each meeting and to give thanks if food is to be consumed. Some groups may like to conclude with a liturgy such as Compline (there are various versions available in prayer books and online: try www.cofe.anglican.org/worship/liturgy/commonworship/texts/daily/night/compline.html).

Other groups may feel more at ease with 'open' prayer, or with an opening prayer and concluding prayer, Lord's Prayer and the Grace. Such prayers may easily be taken or adapted from those offered at the end of each chapter of this book. It does not matter how you do it, but please make sure that you pray and give thanks in any event. 'Whether you eat or drink, or whatever you do, do everything for the glory of God' (1 Corinthians 10:31).

1 John Gray, *Heresies: Against Progress and Other Illusions* (Granta, 2004), p. 35.

2 See UNICEF, *Child Poverty in Perspective: An Overview of Child Well-Being in Rich Countries*, Feb 2007

3 Cathy C. Campbell, *Stations of the Banquet* (Liturgical Press, 2003), p. 61.

4 Mike Appleby, *What Should We Do about Animal Welfare?* (Blackwell, 1999), p. 3.

5 See *Report of the Committee to Consider the Ethical Implications of Emerging Technologies in the Breeding of Farm Animals* (HMSO, 1995).

6 Tom Harpur, *The Spirituality of Wine* (Northstone, 2004), p. 6.

7 Wilfred Thesiger, *Arabian Sands* (Motivate Publishing, 1994), p. 148.

8 See Ahmed Osman, *Stranger in the Valley of the Kings: Solving the Mystery of an Ancient Egyptian Mummy* (Harper & Row, 1987).

9 See www.arkdiscovery.com/joseph.htm

10 See Miriam Feinberg Vamosh, *Food at the Time of the Bible* (Abingdon Press, 2004), p. 72.

11 L. Shannon Jung, *Food for Life: The Spirituality and Ethics of Eating* (Fortress Press, 2004), p. 120.

12 Vamosh, *Food at the Time of the Bible*, p. 72

13 See Melvin Kranzberg, *The Siege of Paris, 1870–1871: A Political and Social History* (Greenwood Press, 1950), p. 63.

14 For an account of this, see John Gray, *Al Qaeda and What It Means to Be Modern* (Faber and Faber, 2003), p. 62.

15 Jung, *Food for Life*, p. 67.

16 Harpur, *The Spirituality of Wine*, p. 109.

17 See *Agricultural Outlook*, July 1997 (Economic Research Service, US Department of Agriculture). See also www.ers.usda.gov/publications/agoutlook/jul1997

18 See Office of National Statistics, *Family Spending* (Palgrave Macmillan, 2007). See also:
www.statistics.gov.uk/StatBase/Product.asp?vlnk=361

19 Rex Russell, MD, *What the Bible Says about Healthy Living* (Regal Books, 1999), p. 92.

20 Vamosh, *Food at the Time of the Bible*, p. 27.

21 Harpur, *The Spirituality of Wine*, p. 18.

22 Robert J. Karris, *Eating Your Way through Luke's Gospel* (Liturgical Press, 2006), p. 97.

23 Sue Hookway, *The Miracles of Jesus* (Bible Society, 2006).

24 See Eric-Peter Lipson, *Passover Haggadah: A Messianic Celebration* (Purple Pomegranate, 2nd Edition, 1988), p. 9.

25 See Ceil and Moishe Rosen, *Christ in the Passover: Why Is This Night Different?* (Moody Press, 1978), p. 52.

26 Melito of Sardis, 'On Pascha and Fragments' (ed. G.S. Hall) quoted in *Jesus* (Oxford Readers), ed. David F. Ford and Mike Higton (OUP, 2002), p. 63.

27 Jean-Anselme Brillat-Savarin (trans. Anne Drayton), *The Philosopher in the Kitchen* (Penguin, 1970), pp. 161–162.